THE GREEN AISLE'S HEALTHY SMOOTHIES AND SLUSHIES

THE GREEN AISLE'S HEALTHY SMOOTHIES AND SLUSHIES

More Than 75 Healthy Recipes to Help You Lose Weight and Get Fit

MICHELLE SAVAGE

Skyhorse Publishing

Contents

Dedication

Bebe, thank you for the comradery during our joint exercise explorations and the companionship you've given me and for exploiting my ineptitude with the ever elusive pull-up.

Scott, I have loved the flights with you; thanks for sharing the stalling lessons and providing me with a means to ensure that my heart is a-okay.

A Note from the Author

On December 27, 2012, I created The Green Aisle to share my passion for cooking and my love of health.

I am a health coach living in California. I enjoy helping others live healthier and happier lives, invigorating their health by educating them on proper nutrition and cooking heart-warming foods that heal the soul and make them feel good about eating. In this book, everything is SkinnyLicious, organic, and wholesome.

Since I have had four cancer surgeries, a severe staph infection, been diagnosed with RV dysplasia and left bundle branch block, suffered from chronic fatigue, overweight, bloated, and distended—all by the age of forty-one—I decided to take a good look at transforming my lifestyle. Nothing is more important than eating clean and healthy, I decided. I am now cancer free, healthy, energetic, full of life, thirty-five pounds lighter, and have enjoyed sharing with you some of the great smoothies and slushies I have created.

Through experimentation and elimination, I was able to create amazing smoothies and slushies that just about anyone can drink, whether you have diabetes, diverticulitis, cancer, or just about any other ailment because these smoothies and slushies are GMO-free, diary-free, sugar-free, soy-free, and gluten-free.

You can now enjoy your all-time favorite treats like strawberry shortcake, zucchini nut bread, strawberry cheese cake, peppermint patties, and much more in a drink that gives your body essential vitamins, nutrients, and enzymes to achieve energy, vitality, and longevity without the guilt, bloating, discomfort or high calorie, sugar-laden foods that give no sustainable nutrients.

I have a passion for sharing empowering information in hopes of inspiring others to continue a healthy lifestyle and attain energy, peace, and balance with organic, raw, all-natural foods.

Have a great day, everyone. I will be in the kitchen, finding new heart-warming foods to share with you! Join www.facebook.com/thegreenaisle.com and check out www.browsethegreenaisle.com for tips to optimal health, detox, weight-loss, and healing recipes.

Introduction

The Essence of Health Begins with the Art of Food

This book is divided into two parts: the informational part is to help you, the reader, make informed decisions regarding your health and well-being. Hopefully, I've taken some of the confusion and guesswork out of this strange new world of healthy living and eating.

Here, I've examined protein powders, milk alternatives, nut butters, and even some healthy substitutions. This is all for your information, and you are free to use any or all of it on the journey to a healthy new you. The second part is the fun and yummy part: smoothies and slushies!

Want to increase your energy levels, enhance metabolism, improve mental clarity, improve digestive function, flush out toxins, and shed a few extra pounds in the process? If so, this book is for you.

Throughout these pages, you'll find eighty-two enticing all natural, **dairy-free**, **soy-free**, **sugar-free**, and **gluten-free** healthy recipes to keep your palate piqued and intrigued. You will also be introduced to some ancient natural superfoods—ingredients that will provide you with vibrant energy and will empower your body, allowing you to feel great and maintain sustainable energy throughout the day.

Practicing a raw lifestyle is simply the best way to give your body the enzymes, vitamins, minerals, natural probiotics, and nutrition it needs to thrive in this toxic environment. Even if you were to consume all-organic produce, environmental factors would continue to invade your body daily from the air you breathe to the products you put on your skin. Your body has been exposed to toxins that wreak havoc on every facet of your health and well-being if you've taken antibiotics, birth control pills, over-the-counter or prescribed medications; used perfume or cologne, fabric softeners, nail polish, bleach, or other cleaning agents; or have amalgam fillings—just to name a few things.

Did you know you can detox your body, build immune function, and even experience weight loss by drinking smoothies and slushies? Blending fruits and vegetables allows the body to retain essential fiber and boosts your overall energy for the day without the stimulants of caffeine or sugar-laden cereals that we have been accustomed to, plus it gives your digestive system the much needed rest it deserves. When fruit and vegetable smoothies are blended, the valuable nutrients are more readily available for your body to absorb, providing hydration, eliminating constipation, lowering cholesterol, stabilizing blood sugars, and preventing cancers and other health-related concerns.

Let's get your body back on track to revitalize and satisfy your hunger with nutrient-dense antioxidants, micronutrients, and enzymes contained in all the Green Aisle's detox smoothies.

In this book, I will share with you the secret to leading an essential and vibrant life: using and feeling natural energy. This pure energy will leave you without the midday crash and will keep you feeling satisfied and fabulous! You will be surprised at how energetic you will feel after just a few days of drinking these fabulous smoothies, and your body will surely thank you for giving it the energy it's been craving.

These easy smoothies can be made in no time so you can keep up with your fast-paced life. This is going to be a great start to a New You! Cheers to a new life full of an abundance of energy and health!

A Clean Protein Source

Some smoothies contained in this book call for a supplemental protein powder. This is a great way to incorporate protein into your diet, especially if you want to limit or eliminate animal protein. But watch, some protein powders on the market may contain ingredients such as soy, dairy, gluten, whey, yeast, artificial flavors and preservatives, added sugars, and/or GMOs.

I recommend using an entirely plant-based hypoallergenic protein source because it's readily digestible and friendly to those who may have food allergens, digestive issues, bloating, gas, or other discomfort. All of these can be painful and even cause life-threatening reactions for some people.

You'll find a variety of amazing plant-based protein powders on the market that provide essential amino acids (BCAAs); some include Vega, Hemp, Sun Warrior, and PlantFusion. These amino acids drive metabolism, build muscle, provide hormonal balance, promote weight loss, increase energy, endurance, and stamina.

When choosing your supplemental protein source, look for ingredients such as pea protein, brown rice protein, or sprouted nuts, seeds, beans, or grains. Be sure to read labels carefully to educate yourself about what you're consuming.

High-Speed Blender

Having a high-speed blender is a must-have in the kitchen and highly recommended for creating top-notch, restaurant style smoothies and improving your health.

The two all-time favorites include the Blendtec and Vitamix. These bad boys are all-in-one high-speed blenders that not only make creamy fruit-and-veggie smoothies, but also nut butters, dips, dressings, nut milks, sauces, baby food, ice cream, creamy soups, and more.

When you put your favorite ingredients into the blender (I use Blendtec), it automatically speeds up and slows down, then shuts off when the cycle is complete. This way, your smoothie recipes turn out perfect every time—in only forty seconds. With its user-friendly design, clean-up is quick and easy. The blender also fits easily under most cabinetry.

Toxins, Free Radicals & Enzymes

Foods containing high levels of acidic qualities can easily exhaust the body and destroy bones, creating many health concerns, depleting sodium, potassium, magnesium, and calcium—making persons prone to chronic and degenerative disease.

According to Peter Shepherd, founder of Trans4mind.com, the body will borrow from vital organs and bones to buffer (neutralize) the acid and safely remove it from your body. This continued strain will cause the body to suffer severely and cause prolonged damage. This may be evident in symptoms including: body aches and pains, headaches, insomnia, fatigue, heartburn, bloating, cancers—high levels of acidic blood have been proven present in all patients who have been diagnosed with cancer—stomach problems, diabetes, obesity, disease, and other underlying effects that go undetected for years. The root cause is tissue acid waste in the body.

Upon entering the bloodstream, pathogens and toxins are carried first to the liver and then to the other organs throughout the body. Nutritional deficiencies and/or toxic overload may impair the ability of the liver to filter out these toxins. Thus causing the toxins instead to be stored and, in time, initiate chronic disease.

After consistently indulging in processed and unhealthy food, your body's digestive system becomes overworked, making it nearly impossible to fully break down and absorb all the essential enzymes and nutrients it was designed to. This poor digestion can create constipation, foul-smelling or frequent gas, bloating, discomfort, distention, and weight gain.

Toxic buildup within the body is the primary cause of epidemics, diseases, and ill health. These toxins are called free radicals, which are damaging to the inside of the body, destroying enzymes. Enzymes are essential for breathing, kidney and liver function, and digestion. When there is a decline of enzymes, the foods consumed are not completely broken down, which causes food to sit undigested, fermenting, causing discomfort, gas, bloating, and other problems.

If you're feeling sluggish or have many health issues, you're living in a toxic body. If the body has a strong odor, this is a sign that free radicals are flourishing. If the body is storing fat, this is a sign that free radicals are doing damage. These damaging toxins are fat soluble, which means they readily combine and react with fatty tissue, and continue to build their destructive path, causing more cellular damage and more fat, aging the body faster, and creating a decline in quality of life.

There are a few steps you can do to help detoxify your body, eliminate bloating and discomfort after meals, jump-start your weight-loss goals, and boost your energy levels. This is what makes this smoothie book stand out from the rest. We weren't given a handbook on the art of food, and many don't even know the dangers that can go hand-in-hand with the typical American diet. Take the time to read these helpful tips before starting your smoothie journey. Your body will thank you!

Probiotics

Pro and *biota* = for life. Probiotics are an everyday essential bacteria of live organisms used to aid in re-establishing and balancing the micro flora in the gut. You may think bacteria are bad, but there are trillions of essential bacteria that our body already has and needs to boost our immunity, guard against harmful bacteria, aid in the digestion of food, and keep our intestines healthy, along with utilizing B vitamins to help your system become stronger.

Taking medications and antibiotics can lower the friendly bacteria the body needs to be in a state of good health. This is why I've created a great strawberry cheesecake, chocolate cheesecake, and a few other tasty smoothies. You can have all the goodness of these treat-like smoothies while building beneficial bacteria to aid in creating a state of good health again. Being healthy never tasted so good!

The Skinny on Dairy and Soy

Start by omitting dairy from your diet. The milk we consume is full of pesticides, hormones, antibiotics, and IGF1—an insulin growth factor hormone—that not only promotes the growth of normal tissues, like bones, but also promotes the growth of abnormal tissues, like cancer, and ages the body faster. Plus, the calcium and phosphorus found in milk blocks the absorption of iron in the body, leaving you fatigued and sluggish throughout the day.

Soybeans

In the United States, 95 percent of soy has been genetically modified (GMO: genetically modified organism) by injecting a gene into the plant that creates a resistance to the pesticide Round-Up. When these heavy doses of pesticides are sprayed over the crops, the weeds and all other plants die except the genetically modified soy. Most of the ill effects of consuming this soy are linked with thyroid disease, digestive problems, reproductive disorders, cancer, and other major diseases; it also contains a neurotoxin that may lead to neurological damage in the brain.

These toxic soybeans undergo a process through an aqueous alcohol (methanol, ethanol and isopropyl alcohol) wash to create a by-product used as a flavor enhancer and food additive which is lurking in many processed foods on the market today: power bars, protein powders, infant formula, veggie burgers, soups, baked goods, and many other foods.

This additive may be listed under different ingredient labels; such as natural flavor, hydrolyzed soy protein, soybean oil, and soy lethicin just to name a few.

If choosing soy products, look for "certified non-GMO," and be sure to read labels carefully to educate yourself about what you're consuming.

Milk Alternatives

Switching to homemade coconut or other nut milk is a great alternative and easy to make. Just make sure the nuts are organic. Some store-bought nuts go through a bleaching process and, therefore, contain toxins.

Buying store-bought brand coconut and nut milks are convenient, but notice the other ingredients, chemicals, preservatives, and natural flavors. To take the guess work out of conventional store-bought brands, coconut and nut milks can be made easily at home and are a whole lot cheaper.

Nut Milk Recipe

Almonds contain vitamin E, calcium, phosphorous, iron, potassium, folic acid, magnesium, zinc, selenium, copper, niacin, riboflavin, and potassium. They help boost energy, prevent heart attacks, regulate blood pressure, reduce fatty plaque on arteries, and contain mono-saturated fat protein. They also contain antioxidants to reduce the risk of heart disease and are rich in fiber, help prevent constipation, offer protection from diabetes, regulate cholesterol, reduce the risk of Alzheimer's, regulate blood pressure, and are good for the heart and brain.

Ingredients
1 cup of preferred nut: almond, cashew, Brazil, hazelnut, etc.
4–6 dates, pitted (optional)
Half the beans of a vanilla pod or
1 teaspoon alcohol-free vanilla extract (optional)
Pinch of sea salt
4 cups water

Directions
Soak one cup of preferred nuts and pitted dates overnight in water. Drain and rinse the nuts the next morning. This allows the release of enzyme inhibitors.

Once the enzyme inhibitors are released, the nut seeds are now enlivened. This is the key to obtaining enzyme-rich nuts into your diet to get the benefits that can help you feel invigorated.

Place the rinsed nuts into a high-speed blender along with all other ingredients. You can use two cups of water for a rich whole milk flavor or more water, depending on the consistency you prefer.

Blend until creamy, about 1 to 2 minutes; times may vary depending on the blender you use.

Place a mesh strainer over a glass bowl and pour in the nut mixture and allow it to drain. Allow the milk to drain thoroughly, and shake the strainer a bit to allow the remaining drops of milk to drain into the bowl. To yield more milk, use a cheese cloth and pour the milk into it, squeezing out the liquid thoroughly.

Pour the nut milk into a glass container, preferably a mason jar, place the lid, and store in your refrigerator for up to five days. Just make sure to give it a little shake before each use.

Coconut Milk Recipe

Coconuts get a bad rap for their saturated fat, but healthy fats are essential to dietary needs, unlike trans fats, which are contained in dairy and animal fats. Coconuts can have many useful benefits, aiding in immune function, reduction of heart disease, and weight loss. Weight loss, really? Yes. Persons who include some healthy fats in their diet curb appetite, satiate sugar cravings, stay full longer, increase metabolism, and tend to stay thin. Coconut milk has antibacterial and antiviral properties, which aid in the fight against viruses and bacteria.

Ingredients
1 cup coconut meat
1 cup coconut water
1 cup water

Directions
Open a fresh young coconut by using the back end of a meat cleaver. Place the coconut on the counter on its side.

Tap with the non-sharp end of a meat cleaver along the top section of the coconut. Tap and turn the coconut, rotating the coconut all the way around until you have completely tapped the whole coconut.

Pull the coconut apart at the perforated areas. Pour the coconut water into a mason jar and store in your refrigerator. Coconut water contains essential electrolytes, a great add-in for smoothies.

Use a spoon to scrape out the coconut meat.

Place 1 cup coconut meat, 1 cup water, and 1 cup coconut water, depending on your preferred consistency, into a blender and blend until creamy.

That's all it takes to make homemade coconut milk. Store in your refrigerator for up to five days.

You may opt to strain your coconut milk if you do not have a high-speed blender and have chunks of coconut meat left in your milk.

Bonus Recipe: Young Thai Coconut Milk

Ingredients
1 fresh young Thai coconut*

Directions
Open the young Thai coconut and pour the coconut water into a high speed blender. Scoop out all of the soft coconut meat and place it in the blender with the coconut water.

Blend in a high speed blender for 45 seconds until creamy; pour into a clean dry mason jar and store in the refrigerator.

For a thinner milk, add ¼ cup water at a time until you reach desired consistency.

*1 fresh young Thai coconut yields approximately 1½ to 2 cups of coconut water and ½ to 1 cup of coconut meat; use everything you can get out of the coconut.

Want a quick way to open your coconut in just seconds? I love my Coco-Jack! It's one investment that keeps on giving. Just go to coco-jack.com, place your order, and type INDULGE in the discount code box.

Bonus Recipe: Creamy Coconut Popsicles

Coconut popsicles are a great way to kick the summer off right, whether you're off to the beach or ready for a BBQ in the backyard. Plus, you can add your choice of fruit to the mix. The flavors are virtually endless and so easy to make. The kiddos will be ecstatic.

Ingredients
2 cups coconut milk
½ cup of your favorite fruit: raspberries, blueberries, strawberries, kiwi, etc. (optional)
1 tablespoon agave or honey (optional)
2 ice pop trays
24 popsicle sticks

Directions
Blend coconut milk, agave or honey, and your favorite fruit for 40 seconds or until smooth.

Or you may opt to chop your fruit or slice it thinly and add it to your milk for a sweet creation that your friends and family will enjoy.

Just pour milk, or milk with fruit option, between ice pop molds and freeze for 1 hour. Insert sticks and continue to freeze until frozen solid, at least 4 hours.

Bonus Recipe: Coconut Whipped Cream (nondairy whipped cream)

Ingredients
1 cup coconut cream*

½ teaspoon vanilla bean powder or 1 teaspoon alcohol-free vanilla extract
2 tablespoons agave

Directions
Blend coconut cream, vanilla, and agave in a large mixing bowl with an electric mixer until light and fluffy peaks of cream form. Eat immediately or refrigerate until it's time for dessert. Want to get a little fancy? Fill a piping bag with cooled coconut whipped cream and swirl over warm cocoa, smoothies, or desserts. But be warned, this sweet coconut whipped cream is extremely addicting!

*1 can organic coconut milk where the only ingredients are coconut, water, and guar gum. Each can contains approximately one cup of coconut cream. Keep the can in the coldest part of the refrigerator until use. Do not shake the can or the cream and liquid will emulsify; we want to keep it separated. After opening, carefully scoop the cream from the top of the can and reserve the liquid for smoothies, if desired.

What's in Your Peanut Butter?

Most traditional name-brand peanut butter and nut butters that are sold nationwide include sugar, partially hydrogenated vegetable oil (rapeseed, cottonseed, soybean), and salt. The ingredients listed can do more harm than good. Partially hydrogenated oils have been banned by European countries for the high concentration of trans fatty acids, which are directly related to the development of diabetes, cancer, and cardiovascular disease. Hydrogenated oil is used for the sole purpose of prolonging the shelf life of processed foods.

The sugar additive lowers immunity and robs bones of essential minerals and offers no nutritional value, is highly addictive, and robs your body of energy, creates acidic blood, raises blood sugar levels, contributes to obesity, eczema, aging, and arthritis.

Table salt mimics the taste of naturally occurring sea salt, but is a manufactured form of sodium called sodium chloride and may contain sodium bicarbonate, fluoride, bleach, MSG, and aluminum derivatives, among other things, which can be toxic. Natural salt is cooked at extreme temperatures and loses the important elements that naturally occur in sea salt; thus making our bodies feel dehydrated. It can also cause high blood pressure, diabetes, gout, edema, and weight gain.

Unlike table salt, natural sea salt is not chemically treated. It is obtained by naturally evaporating seawater. It contains essential minerals, such as iron, magnesium, calcium, potassium, zinc, and iodine. The natural minerals help the body stay hydrated, regulate heartbeat and blood pressure, improve brain function, alkalize the body, provide electrolyte balance, and boost the creation of digestive enzymes, all of which has the ability to detoxify and heal the body and is vital for vibrant health.

With all this said, why buy store-bought brand nut butters, when nut butters can be made easily at home with all wholesome natural ingredients?

Nut Butter

Ingredients
1 cup preferred nut: Almonds, cashews, peanuts
2 tablespoons coconut, walnut, or olive oil
½ teaspoon sea salt

Directions
Soak nuts for 2 hours or preferably overnight. Drain, rinse, and place nuts on a cookie sheet to dry.

Melt 1 to 2 tablespoons of coconut oil to liquid form. Add nuts and 1 teaspoon of sea salt in blender and pulsate the blender a few times. Use a spatula to scrape the mixture back to the bottom of the blender, and continue this process until you have the consistency of peanut butter you desire, whether chunky or creamy. You may opt to add 1–2 additional tablespoons of your preferred oil until you reach your desired consistency.

Bonus Recipe: Toasted Honey Peanut Butter

Ingredients
1½ cups raw shelled peanuts

¼ cup olive oil or peanut oil
2 teaspoons honey*
¹/₈–¼ teaspoon sea salt

Directions

Dry roast the raw peanuts in a nonstick skillet over medium-low heat for approximately 8 minutes; tossing occasionally so peanuts don't burn. This allows the peanuts to sweat out natural oils. If the peanuts start to blacken to quickly or pop in the skillet, turn down the heat to a slow toast.

Transfer toasted peanuts into a high speed blender for a smooth peanut butter or food processor for a bit more chunky consistency. Blend for 30 seconds, then add olive oil and continue to blend 30 more seconds. Add honey and sea salt and continue to blend 30 more seconds. Use a spatula to scrape the mixture back to the bottom of the blender, if necessary.

Continue this process for up to a total of 5 minutes; then you will see a natural toasted honey peanut butter so good you'll be eating it with a spoon.

Use a silicon spatula to scrape the peanut butter into a four ounce mason jar, place lid and store in the refrigerator for up to one month. It can also be stored in the cupboard; oils may separate over time, so give it a little whirl with your spoon before consuming.

*Vegan option; maple syrup

Meat Dangers

Slowly eliminate the consumption of meats, especially lunch meats or processed meats and hot dogs. If you're having trouble cutting back on meats, at least stick to a portion that is no bigger than the palm of your hand, lean and grass-fed.

Processed meats contain large amounts of sodium nitrates, which convert to nitrosamines in the stomach. Sodium nitrate is a chemical compound that may cause cancer and change the structure of your DNA.

Manufacturers are allowed to limit a certain amount of sodium nitrate to products consumed because of its known causes in the development of cancer, as per the report in the July 2009 issue of the *American Journal of Clinical Nutrition*. Per the National Institutes of Health, in areas where consumption of high sodium nitrate intake is shown, persons have reported to have more cancers. Sodium nitrate is used to stabilize the colors in meat and prevent the growth of toxin botulism, also allowing the product to have a longer shelf life.

If inhaling sodium nitrate in dust form will cause respiratory problems, shortness of breath, and coughing, and if sodium nitrate can cause redness, itching, and irritation if applied directly to the skin, why ingest it? By ingesting sodium nitrate, this can cause headaches, stomach discomfort, and many other problems, according to the National Institutes of Health's US National Library of Medicine, studies from the University of Minnesota Extension website, and Natural News.

Ditch the Bean

The coffee bean, that is. It is acidic, toxic soup. Coffee consumption prevents the absorption of critical vitamins and minerals into the body. The polyphenols contained in coffee block the body's ability to absorb iron, making you feel fatigued, resulting in less physical performance and slower immune function. Iron is an essential mineral that helps transport oxygen throughout the body and gives the body energy.

Caffeine spikes cortisol levels. Just one cup of coffee can spike those levels for up to 14 to 18 hours. High cortisol levels make it very difficult to lose weight. Yes, you'll get a jolt of energy and feel better, but the effects are temporary. After the caffeine wears off, you may experience anxiety, joint pains, and brain fog.

This does not apply to the green coffee bean extract. This extract, on the one hand, has not been roasted or processed and has less caffeine, but there is controversy about other ingredients added to these supplements, like fillers and flow agents. Read labels carefully.

Effects Coffee Has on Your Digestion

When coffee beans are roasted, some of the chlorogenic acid compounds, which aid in the slow release of glucose (sugar) into your bloodstream, are destroyed. This can increase weight gain. The percentage of higher decomposition exists in cheaper brands of coffee.

Coffee is very acidic in nature, and excessive coffee consumption can wreak havoc on your stomach, causing gastroesophageal reflux disease—GERD—which can increase gastric ulcers and increase gastric cancer, according to the 2006 *Methods and Findings in Experimental and Clinical Pharmacology Journal*.

Coffee leads to dehydration and loss of nutrients. With this combination, the body will age faster, creating more wrinkles, and causing fatigue, not to mention the "caffeine crash."

The United States has admitted that coffee has been found to contain formaldehyde and styrene in addition to unknown chemical agents, which come from foam coffee cups and carry-out containers.

Styrene is used in insulation, automobile parts, drinking cups, carpet backing, etc., according to the Agency for Toxic Substances and Disease Registry. Workers in industries that use this chemical to reinforce plastics are at a higher risk of exposure, leading to damaged white blood cells or lymphocytes, and are at a higher risk to develop cancers, per the Report on Carcinogens, prepared by the National Toxicology Program, part of the US National Institutes of Health.

Formaldehyde is a widely used flammable and colorless preservative used to make resins for household items, including plastics, textile finishes, paper product coatings, and preservative in mortuaries and some hair straightening products.

Per the US Department of Health and Human Services, these can also be included in foam coffee cups and carry-out containers:

- Riddelline—causing liver tumors in rats
- Ortho-Nitrotoluene—a clear, water-insoluble liquid, sweet smelling, occurs naturally in crude oil, used in solvents, paints, paint thinners, fingernail polish, lacquers, adhesives, rubber, and inhaling toluene can cause severe neurological harm
- Cobalt-tungsten carbide—powder or hard metal form
- Aristolochic acid—a carcinogen

There are more than 240 substances contained in these foam coffee cups and carry-out containers. Just a few of the many toxins mentioned above give an idea of what you can be consuming and not even know it.

Are the risks worth it? The next time you go to your local gas station or the convenient fast-food restaurants for a cup of joe, think of what you are really about to ingest: toxic soup.

Is Coffee Really Toxic?

This is a controversial subject. Studies often do not take into account that mycotoxins are almost always contained within processed coffee beans. Mycotoxins, the molds that grow on coffee beans during processing, are just one of many compounds that may cause health problems, such as cardiomyopathy, cancer, kidney disease, and brain damage. This toxin is the compound that makes your coffee taste bitter. So you add sugar, cream, and syrups, which, in turn, can create other problems with your overall health.

Researchers have found that most low-quality brand coffee contains 52 to 91.7 percent of this mycotoxin compound. The coffee food supply is one of the largest sources of these toxins. Along with these research studies, ochratoxin A has been found in coffee, a toxin that targets your kidneys, causes cancer, and compromises the immune function and nervous system.

Is Decaf Better?

You may think decaffeinated coffee is better. Well, think again. Caffeine deters *some* molds and organisms from growing on the beans itself while stored, but when the caffeine is removed, the levels of ochratoxin and aflatoxin are higher.

During the processing of coffee, growers allow beans to sit in vats of water and ferment so the outer parts of the bean are more easily removed. This creates toxins.

Some articles claim coffee can lower risks of strokes, can improve focus and performance, and is an antioxidant by the Standard American Diet. But keep in mind that coffee is acidic and not in line with the goals of a healthy lifestyle. Coffee consumption creates:

- Caffeine dependency
- Yellow teeth
- Gastrointestinal and stomach problems
- Psychological effects and sleep changes
- High cholesterol
- High blood pressure
- Negative effects on pregnancy
- Iron deficiency, anemia

Now, Do You Want to Kick the Coffee Habit But Just Don't Know How?

You don't have to feel like you're going cold turkey. I've got two amazing recipes that are organic, natural, and chemical-free. They are non-acid forming, which helps restore alkalinity and balance to the body, providing energy from natural nutrients and not stimulants and taste just as good as a Starbucks Mocha Frappuccino but without all the added calories.

Hot Coffee

This organic drink contains 48 milligrams of potassium, soluble fiber, and 390 milligrams of insulin that comes from chicory root, which supports beneficial micro flora in the gut and creates intestinal health.

These are all natural organic ingredients. Carob, barley, chicory, and Ramon nuts are nutrient-rich foods of the Maya civilization that are roasted and ground to brew and taste like coffee, without the caffeine crash.

Ingredients
1 cup water
1 Teeccino Herbal coffee pouch
1 tablespoon of cocoa powder
Dash of almond or coconut milk
3 drops of liquid Stevia, agave or honey
Nondairy whipped cream

Directions
Boil water and pour into a coffee mug. Add 1 herbal coffee bag and dip the bag a few times for the best brew.

Place a small plate on top of your mug for 1 to 2 minutes to steep.

Add cocoa powder, a dash of almond or coconut milk, your desired sweetener, and stir. Top it off with nondairy whipped cream, if preferred, and maybe a dash of cinnamon.

Java Junkie

Wow, you're not going to believe this rush! The combination of the moringa, maca, and matcha will jump-start your morning with tons of energy, which will keep you focused and on the top of your game. This is a great smoothie if you're trying to wean yourself off coffee. Matcha contains natural caffeine, while the moringa is an abundant plant source with essential vitamins, amino acids, and forty-six antioxidants to help fight free radicals and increase metabolism. Maca will increase strength and energy with a bonus sexual enhancement.

Ingredients
1 tablespoon chocolate protein powder
¼ teaspoon moringa powder
½ teaspoon maca
½ teaspoon matcha green tea powder
½ teaspoon cocoa powder
1 cup cashew milk
1 tablespoon agave
Dash of cayenne

Directions
Blend all ingredients on high for 40 seconds or until smooth and top with nondairy whipped cream, if desired. You may opt to blend the matcha, moringa, and maca in a couple tablespoons of warm water first so that the powders don't clump in your smoothie, especially for those who don't use a high-speed blender.

Water News

Drinking cold water with a meal allows the oils from the food to turn into solids, slowing down the digestion process and causing vessels of the stomach to contract. The now solid oils react with your hydrochloric acids and are absorbed by the intestines faster than your meal, lining your intestines and turning into fats.

While the digestion process has slowed, the food will remain in the stomach longer than it should, fermenting, causing gas, constipation, discomfort, and pain—not allowing nutrients to be absorbed properly.

If you need to drink during a meal, just a sip of warm water will clear the palate. Do not consume a beverage thirty minutes before or after your meal so the gastric acid is not diluted during the digestion process.

The amount of water your body needs depends on many factors, including your health, your weight, how active you are, and where you live.

A good rule of thumb is to drink half your body weight in fluid ounces. For example, let's say, if you are 140 pounds, consuming 70 ounces of water a day is ideal.

Water is important to flush out toxins from vital organs, carry nutrients to cells, and provide a moist environment for your ears, nose, and throat tissues. Inadequate water supply can lead to dehydration and lead to feeling fatigued.

Benefits of Drinking Lemon Water
- Boosts immune system
- Relieves coughs, allergies, and asthma
- Helps with weight loss
- Balances pH
- Aids in digestion
- Diuretic
- Clears skin

Start each day with one cup of hot water, 1 tablespoon of lemon juice, 1 teaspoon pink Himalayan salt, and/or a dash of cayenne pepper.

Chewing and Digestion

If you chow down in a hurry or only chew a few times before swallowing your foods, you can greatly increase digestive problems. Take your time and enjoy the flavors. Chewing thoroughly, twenty to thirty times, will allow digestive enzymes the ability to break down food properly so your digestive tract doesn't have to work so hard. This will allow the nutrients to convert to energy more readily and speed up the digestive process. When food is not properly broken down, it can create constipation, indigestion, and an overgrowth of bacteria in the colon.

Raw Vegan Food Pyramid

Get your greens on! That's right, greens. The majority of persons on the typical American diet don't get enough veggies. The FDA-approved food pyramid shows three to four servings of vegetable and fruit and six to eleven servings of bread, cereal, rice, and pasta are appropriate for a well-balanced diet. Wow! This is a train wreck. If you start your morning with the typical pancake, toast, or cereal, you are lowering your pH, converting carbs to sugars, and lowering your daily energy.

The best alkalizing food pyramid would be:

- Leafy greens, which are chock-full of nutrients
- Fruits and vegetables, which are loaded with vitamins and good carbohydrates to fuel your body
- Sprouts and legumes, which are a powerhouse of nutrients
- Grains, quinoa, buckwheat, wild, and brown rice
- Nuts and seeds, which are a great source of protein (nuts are higher in fat, so limit the amount consumed) and include flax, sesame, pumpkin, hemp, and other seeds
- Herbs, microgreens, and wheatgrass
- Fermented foods, which will reestablish gut flora
- Sea vegetables, which are loaded with tons of minerals
- Nutritional yeast, which is great source of vitamin B12 and give recipes a cheesy flavor

Veggies should be the prime source of your diet. If you're not used to eating your veggies, try a few of the vegetable-based smoothies contained in this book to start. They are alkalizing, fresh live greens that contain a high pH balance, chlorophyll, and powerful enzymes essential for sustainable life!

Buying and Prepping Produce

Organic Labels

Buy organic, if possible, to limit the amount of toxins and pesticides in your produce. Make sure the label bears the seal USDA. Many organic products are misleading. If the label reads "100 percent organic," you are assured that it is just that. Some labels may read "organic." This means that 95 percent of the product must be organic. Labels that read "made with organic ingredients" mean you are only getting 70 to 95 percent organic.

Some produce should absolutely be bought organic, as they contain the most pesticides. This list includes corn, apples, celery, peaches, strawberries, blueberries and other berries, tomatoes, spinach, kale, collard greens, grapes, and lettuces.

The rule is, if the vegetable or fruit has a thin skin, avoid nonorganic, if at all possible. If the produce has a thicker skin and you are purchasing it nonorganic, you will need to remove the skin or peel it first. This list includes such items as cucumbers, avocado, pineapples, kiwi, cantaloupe, lemon, limes, watermelon, and grapefruit.

PLU Numbers (Price-Look Up Code)

Notice the labels of fruits and vegetables in your supermarket and know what they mean. You will know if the produce is organic when the label starts with the PLU number 9. You will be rest assured that your food is healthier and nutritious and does not contain fertilizer or dangerous toxins.

Produce label numbers that start with 8 are GMOs. Never purchase GMO produce. The American Academy of Environmental Medicine urges doctors to prescribe non-GMO diets to protect their patients, citing the toxic insecticide used during farming causes organ damage, immune system disorders, and gastrointestinal problems; it ages the body faster and creates infertility.

Label numbers that start with 3 or 4 are conventionally grown, and growers could have sprayed pesticides on them. *Conventionally grown* seems a bit elusive and tends to portray normal and/or safe. On the contrary, conventionally grown produce may contain harmful toxins that will destroy our health.

Wash All Produce

It is extremely important to wash all fruits and vegetables before consuming. They can harbor bacteria or other contaminants, such as E. coli or parasites.

After bringing your produce home, spray everything with a veggie wash or a homemade wash made of vinegar and lemon, place in a clean sink or tub, and fill with filtered clean water. Tap water is not going to work; it can contain carcinogens, like arsenic and other contaminants that can seep into your produce. Let produce sit in wash and clean water for up to 15 to 20 minutes. Then scrub and rinse.

You will notice after soaking that the remaining water is full of dirt and other debris. Just imagine if you hadn't washed them properly beforehand what you would be consuming. Plus, the taste of the produce after cleaning will be more pleasant. They will yield essential vitamins and minerals that will be more readily absorbed into the body if no toxins reside.

Prep Fruits and Veggies

When preparing frozen fruits, peel bananas first and cut into halves before freezing. If this is not done, the frozen banana peel will turn brown and will be extremely difficult to take off. Strawberries should be hulled before freezing. If the stems are still intact, it is almost impossible to cut them off when frozen. Any fruit containing seeds or stems should have them removed first before freezing. Also, to save the life of your blender—especially if you don't have a high-speed blender—first chop hard vegetables, like carrots, celery, etc., into smaller pieces.

Don't Forget to Soak Your Nuts!

It is essential to soak nuts, especially almonds, for proper digestion. Raw almonds contain tannic acid, which is an enzyme inhibitor that protects the nut until the proper environment and moisture conditions are reached to allow the nut to germinate. Eating the nut before it releases its enzyme inhibitors will make it more difficult to digest and limit nutrients your body can absorb.

Soaking your nuts for seven to twelve hours is preferred. The next morning, drain and rinse. Presoaked nuts can be refrigerated for up to a week. Storing moist nuts may produce mold over time, so if you intend to keep the nuts as fresh as possible and keep a longer shelf life, you can dry them in a dehydrator for twelve to twenty-four hours or until crisp. If you do not have a dehydrator, you can dry them in your oven at 150 to 200 degrees until dry. Nuts are more nutritious when soaked and, when dried, the crisp texture is scrumptious for snacking, especially when sea salt is added before the drying process.

SMOOTHIE AND SLUSHIE RECIPES

Almond Joy

This is a delicious, healthy pick-me-up to keep you from that afternoon slump. Almonds boost energy naturally, regulate blood pressure, reduce risk of heart disease, are good for the heart and brain, aid in the prevention of cancer and constipation, and contain antioxidants, fiber, protein, and omega-3 and -6 fatty acids.

Ingredients
¼ cup of chocolate protein powder
1 cup coconut milk
1 tablespoon cocoa powder
¼ cup of presoaked almonds
½ cup coconut flakes

Directions
Blend all ingredients on high for 40 seconds or until smooth.

Blueberry Boost

Let's crank up the energy! Blueberries contain antioxidants, build the immune system, contain antibacterial properties, and neutralize free radicals.

Ingredients
1½ cups water
1 frozen banana
1 cup frozen blueberries
1 teaspoon honey (optional)

Directions
Blend all ingredients on high for 40 seconds or until smooth.

Beginner Greens

If you're new to green smoothies, this is a great way to begin incorporating all greens without the added fruit. This awesome beginner green smoothie is full of creamy goodness that will have you wanting more. After incorporating the smooth beginner greens like cucumber and celery, you can move on to spinach, kale, watercress, and other greens that will slowly reset your taste buds to crave healthier choices, while you notice sugars, table salt, and processed foods becoming less attractive.

Ingredients
½ lime, juiced
½ cucumber, peeled
8 spinach leaves
1 celery stalk
¼ cup almond milk
¼ avocado
1 mint leaf, chopped
8 ice cubes

Directions
Blend all ingredients on high for 40 seconds or until smooth.

Blueberry Strudel

Want to lower your cholesterol? Gluten-free rolled oats are heart-healthy and cholesterol-lowering. They have the ability to lower LDL and bad cholesterol, prevent the buildup of toxic plaque within the arteries, and promote weight loss by absorbing twenty-five times their volume in liquid, allowing the body to feel full longer, keeping sugar levels at bay, and slowing the digestion rate of carbohydrates by reducing the rate in which sugar can enter the bloodstream.

Ingredients
⅓ cup gluten-free rolled oats
1½ cups almond milk
1 cup frozen blueberries
¼ teaspoon maca
1–2 tablespoons maple syrup

Directions
Soak oats overnight in 1½ cups of almond milk and add to blender with all other ingredients on high for 40 seconds or until smooth.

Broccoli Boost

What a way to get your broccoli in and not even taste it. This little green is packed with calcium, vitamin K, vitamin C, antioxidants to help fight those free radicals, and much, much more. Fuel your great workout and minimize muscle recovery time, build healthy bones, and repair cells with this sweet smoothie.

Ingredients
3 florets of broccoli
1 cucumber
1 green apple, cored and chopped
1 teaspoon agave
1 cup hemp milk
10 ice cubes

Directions
Blend all ingredients on high for 40 seconds or until smooth.

Candied Pumpkin

This incredibly sweet drink will satisfy that sweet tooth currently craving your favorite ice cream, pie, cake, or candy bar. It's so sweet you may not even finish it. How's that for a green drink? Pumpkin seeds are extremely alkaline-forming, which is great for restoring and maintaining health. This little seed will improve bladder function, contains L-tryptophan to fight depression, is high in zinc to protect against osteoporosis, is a natural anti-inflammatory, prevents kidney stone formation, reduces LDL cholesterol, and protects against cancer.

Ingredients
¼ cup pumpkin seeds
1 frozen banana
2 cups spinach
1½ cups coconut water
Dash of cinnamon (optional)

Directions
Presoak pumpkin seeds for 4–6 hours for easy digestion, rinse, and add to blender with all other ingredients on high for 40 seconds or until smooth. Top with cinnamon, if preferred.

Chocolate-Covered Strawberries

Craving chocolate? Enhance your mood and boost those endorphins with cocoa. Did you know one tablespoon of cocoa powder contains only 12.5 calories? This divine chocolate comes from the cocoa bean and is highly nutritious, containing more antioxidants than tea or red wine. No more chocolate bar fix. All you need is a chocolate-covered strawberry smoothie.

Ingredients
1½ cups frozen strawberries
1½ cups almond milk
2 tablespoons chocolate protein powder
1 tablespoon cocoa powder

Directions
Blend all ingredients on high for 40 seconds or until smooth.

Chocolate Cheesecake

Kefir relieves menstrual cramps, enhances liver functioning, promotes blood clotting, increases vitality and longevity, enhances mental clarity, and so much more.

Ingredients
1 cup coconut milk kefir
2 tablespoons peanut butter
1 banana
2 tablespoons coconut flour
2 tablespoons carob
1 teaspoon honey
8 ice cubes

Directions
Blend all ingredients on high for 40 seconds or until smooth.

Cinnamon Toast

A vegan's favorite for a nutty, buttery flavor—nutritional yeast. This is a great replacement for butter on popcorn, soups, and dips. The healthy benefits are tremendous. Just one ounce of nutritional yeast contains 14 grams of protein and 18 amino acids to aid in building muscle, connective tissue, and enzymes, plus metabolize cells for energy.

Why use animal products like cheese, dairy, or butter, when you can get so much more from all natural foods? Nutritional yeast is high in B vitamins, which is essential for the production of red blood cells, insulates nerve cells, and is low in sodium for those monitoring their sodium intake, such as persons with heart disease.

Ingredients
1 frozen banana
1 teaspoon cinnamon
½ cup almond milk
1 teaspoon nutritional yeast
1 tablespoon maple syrup
8 ice cubes

Directions
Blend all ingredients on high for 40 seconds or until smooth.
You may opt to leave the cinnamon out of the smoothie and put a couple cinnamon sticks in its place when you have company for a delectable appeal.

Crazy Chlorophyll

Chlorophyll is highly alkalizing and easily absorbed, delivering oxygen to body tissues and cells, neutralizing toxins, purifying the liver, and improving blood sugar problems. Chlorophyll also contains magnesium, which boosts energy and rebuilds red blood cells. Research has found that cancer is prevented by ingesting chlorophyll. Chlorophyll will kill harmful bacteria, strengthen, rebuild, and replace the body with new tissue, which replenishes the bloodstream.

Ingredients
1 floret of broccoli
3 basil leaves
¼ cucumber
¼ chopped leeks
½ cup arugula and mixed salad greens
1 teaspoon chopped dill
1 cup almond milk
12 ice cubes

Directions
Blend all ingredients on high for 40 seconds or until smooth.

Cucumber Pick-Me-Up

Rosemary is medicine in the organic perfume industry. Consuming this *rosmarius*, which has an antiseptic effect going back to ancient times, relieves abdominal pain, gout, calms the nerves, and alleviates fatigue and anxiety. Burning the branches of rosemary has been practiced in hospitals in France and is used for cleansing the air. Properties of rosemary are abundant from anti-inflammatory, to destroying microorganisms, improving blood flow, and eliminating mind fog. Not only does this fine herb do all these things, but it also increases energy and is a natural antidepressant, revitalizing the body.

Ingredients
1 small Armenian cucumber
½ cup water
1 tablespoon honey
1 teaspoon rosemary
4 key limes, juiced
10 ice cubes

Directions
Blend all ingredients on high for 40 seconds or until smooth.
You may opt to top this smoothie with pine nuts, cayenne pepper, a few green onion whites, and chopped watercress—just something to chew on if you're on a fast.

Dew Delight

Dew your body right by adding this special melon to your diet. This sweet tasting fruit is a summer cuisine, low in calorie and fat, high in fiber, and highly nutritious. The light green pigment is present containing carotenoid and zeaxanthin, which is a powerful antioxidant that helps protect your vision and reduces age-related macular degeneration. Folate is also present in this amazing fruit, guarding against chronic diseases and birth defects. Just one cup of honeydew gives you 12 percent of your daily dose of B6, which metabolizes protein and creates serotonin—a neurotransmitter that regulates mood and promotes a peaceful night's sleep.

Ingredients
1½ cups honeydew melon
4 mint leaves
½ lime, juiced
10 ice cubes

Directions
Blend all ingredients on high for 40 seconds or until smooth.

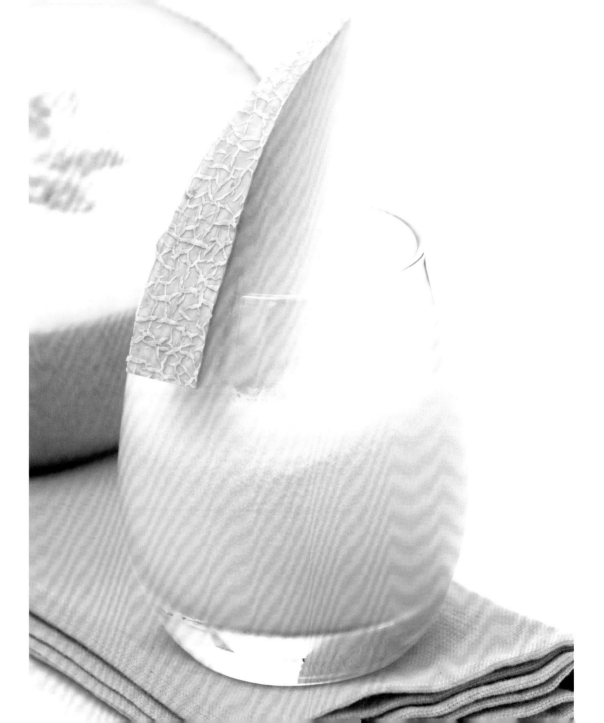

Dew the Fat Burn

The low-glycemic, low-caloric, high water content in honeydew melon will aid in keeping blood sugar levels from spiking, allowing weight loss goals to be achieved easier, and helping you stay full longer. It also reduces the development of type-2 diabetes.

Ingredients
1 cup honeydew melon
2 peeled kiwis
⅓ cup coconut water
4 mint leaves
10 ice cubes

Directions
Blend all ingredients on high for 40 seconds or until smooth.

Fizzy Lime Drop

Kefir means "feel good" in Turkish. It's an enzyme-rich food filled with beneficial microorganisms to balance your inner ecosystem, creating happy micro flora in your gut. Coconut water kefir, has 100 billion probiotic CFUs per one tablespoon. It's a superfood that contains electrolytes identical to those of human blood. It is the best in hydration; has tons of minerals, antioxidants, enzymes, and vitamins; maintains a proper pH; and is one of the best probiotics on the market.

Ingredients

½ cup coconut water kefir
½ cup coconut water
1 lime, juiced
Sliver ginger root
1 tablespoon agave (optional)
8–10 ice cubes

Directions
Blend all ingredients on high for 40 seconds or until smooth. If you are new to coconut water kefir, you may opt to use ¼ cup coconut water kefir and ¾ cup of coconut water until you are used to the flavor.

Go Nuts

Spice up your aphrodisiac with goji. Not only do these cute little red-looking raisins help boost your sex drive, but they are full of protein, essential fatty acids, selenium, antioxidants, carotenoids, iron, zeaxanthin, and lutein, which preserves eyesight. What are you waiting for? Spice up your life a little and Go Nuts.

Ingredients
1 cup hazelnut milk
½ cup goji berries
1 frozen banana

Directions
Blend all ingredients on high for 40 seconds or until smooth.

Grapefruit Twist

Alkaline your diet with grapefruit. With this low-calorie forgotten fruit, you can lower the extra water weight that comes from high-sodium foods, helping you to lose weight faster. It is full of beneficial enzymes that help increase energy and your metabolism.

Ingredients
½ grapefruit, juiced
2 kiwi, peeled
1 lime, juiced
10 ice cubes

Directions
Blend all ingredients on high for 40 seconds or until smooth.

Green Mojito

Mint helps sooth the digestive tract, is great for reducing IBS symptoms, cleanses the stomach, and eliminates toxins.

Ingredients
¼ cucumber
⅓ cup mint leaves, chopped
1 celery sticks
1 lime or ½ lemon, juiced
½ avocado
8 ice cubes
½–1 cup water

Directions
Blend all ingredients on high for 40 seconds or until smooth.

Key Lime Pie

Limes improve gout and urinary disorders, cure scurvy, are anti-aging, and aid in the protection of numerous other ailments. This sour fruit has been used for soft drinks, body oils, cosmetics, hair oils, toothpaste, soaps, disinfectants, and other innumerable products.

Ingredients
1 pitted date
½ cup water
4 tablespoons key lime, juiced
1 cup frozen banana
½ cup almond milk
1 tablespoon vanilla protein powder
1 tablespoon gluten-free rolled oats

Directions
Chop and soak pitted date in ½ cup water for 20 minutes, drain, and add date to blender with all other ingredients on high for 40 seconds or until smooth.

Kiwi Kicker

Kiwi is a water-soluble antioxidant that will kick those free radicals in the butt, improving health and preventing many age-related diseases like macular degeneration.

Ingredients
⅛ cup nut milk
2 kiwi, peeled
1 lime, juiced
½ avocado
⅛ cup walnuts
8 ice cubes

Directions
Blend all ingredients on high for 40 seconds or until smooth.

Longevity Enhancer

This powerful pomegranate antioxidant superfruit has been legendary for centuries, full of compounds and enzymes known to keep bad cholesterol from oxidizing and causing arteriosclerosis or hardening of the arteries. Pomegranates increase oxygen levels to the heart. No more need for over-the-counter aspirin or ibuprofen. Pomegranates keep blood platelets from sticking together, a process that causes blood clots. The antioxidants neutralize free radicals present in the body. You can add pomegranate seeds to any salad. Using these seeds can lower your risk of heart disease and cancer, lessen the symptoms of diarrhea, help with weight loss, and protect against cellular damage.

Ingredients
1 cup pomegranate seeds, juiced
1 red apple, cored and chopped
Handful of grapes
½ cup coconut water
10 ice cubes

Ingredients
Blend all ingredients on high for 40 seconds or until smooth.

Mango Tango

Mangos are rich in pre-biotic dietary fiber, increase metabolic rates, curb appetite, and are rich in antioxidants and phytonutrients.

Ingredients
2 tablespoons of cashew butter
2 oranges, peeled and juiced
1 mango, peeled and pitted
1 nectarine
1 apricot
½ banana
1 teaspoon honey
10 ice cubes

Directions
Blend all ingredients on high for 40 seconds or until smooth.

Peppermint Patty

Bananas are naturally fat- and cholesterol-free, packed with potassium (which helps nerve and muscle function and prevents muscle cramps after an intense workout), B6 (vital to new cell growth), and manganese (for bone health and metabolism).

Ingredients
1 cup nut milk
1 frozen banana
1 tablespoon vanilla protein powder
4 large peppermint leaves, chopped (mint leaves can be substituted)
1 tablespoon cocoa powder
10 ice cubes
6 drops stevia

Directions
Blend all ingredients on high for 40 seconds or until smooth. Top with nondairy creamer, if desired.

Morning Sunrise

Boost your immunity with this Morning Sunrise for protection during the cold and flu season, adding 12 percent of your daily value of calcium, and aiding in strong bones and the prevention of osteoporosis. Oranges contain potassium to aid in the delivery of oxygen to the brain, creating better mental clarity and protecting against daily stressors and depression. They also include thiamine to improve memory.

Ingredients
2 oranges, juiced
1 frozen banana
½ cup almond milk
½ cup presoaked cashews
1 teaspoon honey
1 tablespoon vanilla protein powder
10 ice cubes

Directions
Blend all ingredients on high for 40 seconds or until smooth.

Peach Cobbler

Soothe your tummy with the magic spice of nutmeg. In ancient Chinese medicine, nutmeg has been a staple for treating abdominal pain and inflammation, arthritis, aches, and pains. This special spice is also known to treat halitosis. It rids your mouth from the buildup of bacteria, which is what causes bad breath. Nutmeg detoxifies your liver and kidneys, which is where the buildup of toxins reside. By removing these toxins, it can prevent or dissolve kidney stones and is beneficial for those who have liver disease. These vital organs are extremely important in their role to the body, filtering out waste products from our body and impacting overall health.

Ingredients
1 peach, peeled and pitted
½ teaspoon cinnamon
1 tablespoon vanilla protein powder
½ teaspoon nutmeg
Pinch clove
½ cup almond milk
6 ice cubes

Directions
Blend all ingredients on high for 40 seconds or until smooth. You may opt to save the cinnamon for a garnish on top of the smoothie instead of adding it to the blending process.

Peaches & Cream

Peaches were used in the tenth century by the early Chinese for their properties to extend life. This fruit of goodness is packed with a variety of vitamins and minerals, plus potassium to fight fatigue, anxiety, poor memory, muscle weakness, and much, much more. Popeye could've eaten one peach and gotten as much usable iron as spinach. Not only do peaches contain all this great goodness, but they are 89 percent water, suppress your hunger, and aid in weight loss.

Ingredients
1½ peaches, pitted (peeled optional)
1 banana
1 teaspoon honey
1 tablespoon vanilla protein powder
6 ice cubes

Directions
Blend all ingredients on high for 40 seconds or until smooth.

Pina Colada

Satisfy your sweet cravings with a delicious and nutritious cholesterol-free and fat-free glass of goodness. Pineapples are packed with antioxidants, protecting cells from damaging free radicals that can increase aging and wreak havoc on the body's immunity.

Ingredients
1 scoop vanilla protein powder
1 cup fresh pineapple
1 banana
¾ cup coconut milk
1½ teaspoons vanilla extract
10 ice cubes

Directions
Blend all ingredients on high for 40 seconds or until smooth. Add a slice of pineapple on the side and maybe a cute umbrella, too.

Pink Mojito

This powerhouse of energy is refreshing, hydrating, cancer-fighting, and contains powerful antioxidants called lycopene, which neutralizes free radicals, reducing the severity of asthma, heart disease, and rheumatoid arthritis. Watermelons contain more lycopene than any other fruit or vegetable, as well as vitamin B for energy production, B6 and B1, magnesium, potassium, manganese, and vitamin C and vitamin A.

Ingredients
2 cups seedless watermelon
Handful mint leaves, chopped
1 lime or ½ lemon, juiced
1 tablespoon of honey
10 ice cubes
2 tablespoons sea salt or fine Himalayan pink salt

Directions
Place sea salt on a small plate.
Wet the rim of your glass and press it into sea salt to coat.
Place all other ingredients into a blender on high for 40 seconds or until smooth.
What a refreshing summer treat!

Pumpkin Pie

Pumpkin is rich in vital antioxidants, minerals, and vitamins, has no saturated fat or cholesterol, and contains a powerful kick to keep the heart healthy and waistline in check, scavenging free radicals in the lens of the eye preventing cataracts. It contains zinc to boost immunity and gives bones density support, plus alpha hydroxyl-acids, reducing the signs of aging.

Ingredients
1 cup water
1 cup cooked pumpkin, purèed
1 scoop vanilla protein powder
Dash pumpkin spice
Dash of nutmeg and clover are optional—if you like more, POW!
Dash of cinnamon
8 ice cubes

Directions
Blend all ingredients on high for 40 seconds or until smooth. Top with nondairy creamer, if desired.

Blackberry Pie

Heart healthy blackberries are high in potassium and fiber, which aids in promoting cardiovascular health and lowering cholesterol levels, creating a great source of antioxidant flavonoids and manganese, which relax arteries and blood vessels. Blackberries are also high in vitamin C, which reduces uric acid levels in the blood to help prevent gout.

Ingredients
1 cup black seedless grapes
1 cup blackberries
1 tablespoon vanilla protein powder
1 teaspoon maca
1 teaspoon agave
½ cup almond milk
1 teaspoon coconut oil, melted
12 ice cubes

Directions
Blend all ingredients on high for 40 seconds or until smooth.

Raspberry Tart

Promote weight loss with this natural sweetness, curbing your cravings for less wholesome foods like fast-food burgers. Boost your enzymes to alleviate free radicals and inflammation instead of going for the over-the-counter ibuprofen or aspirin. This little fruit contains a large amount of antioxidants to fight aging and slow cancer growth. According to an article by the Cancer Prevention Research Center, the ellagic acid found in raspberries, a phenolic compound, kills many types of cancers.

Ingredients
½ cup raspberries
½ cup blueberries
1 tablespoon agave
10 ice cubes

Directions
Blend all ingredients on high for 40 seconds or until smooth.

Sea Monster

Kombu's amazing health benefits include essential trace minerals of vitamin B12 and vitamin D. Kombu detoxifies the body by binding to heavy metals and expels toxins from the body. It also protects against gamma radiation, aids in digestion, improves blood circulation, prevents constipation, balances alkaline and acid in the body, contributes to the prevention of cancer by leveling pH balance, aids in a stronger nervous system, and helps the absorption of calcium in the body.

Ingredients
2 inches of Kombu
1 cup coconut water
1 frozen banana

Directions
Soak Kombu in 1 cup coconut water for 1 hour, then pour into blender with all other ingredients on high for 40 seconds or until smooth.

Season Cider

An apple a day, 'tis the season for keeping the doctor away. Green apples are nutrient-rich, low-calorie, and have a natural sweetness packed with minerals to purify the blood, relieve constipation, reduce high blood pressure, and stabilize blood sugar levels while providing sustainable energy and controlling hunger.

Ingredients
1 green apple, cored and chopped
1 cup hazelnut milk
½ teaspoon maca
½ frozen banana
¼ teaspoon nutmeg
1 teaspoon cinnamon (optional)
10 ice cubes

Directions
Blend all ingredients on high for 40 seconds or until smooth.

Sour Apple

Want to improve your cognitive function and memory? The omega-3 fatty acids in hemp milk allow the neurons in your brain to communicate effectively. Even though hemp milk is derived from the hemp seed, the plant that produces marijuana, this milk doesn't contain the active ingredient THC. It has more calcium than cow's milk, plus is packed full of iron, potassium, zinc, phosphorus, riboflavin, niacin, vitamins A, E, B12, folic acid, thiamin, omega-6 and omega-3 fatty acids, fiber, protein, and ten essential amino acids.

Ingredients
1 green apple, cored and chopped
1 kiwi, peeled if not organic
1 lime, peeled
1 cup hemp milk
10 ice cubes

Directions
Blend all ingredients on high for 40 seconds or until smooth.

South of the Border

Antioxidants far superior to fruits or vegetables are found in cumin. It has been used to promote well-being for years in numerous diseases and disorders, helping to boost immunity, increase metabolism and absorption of nutrients, aid in digestion, the reduction of hypoglycemia, and treatment of asthma, colds, anemia, skin disorders, and cancer.

Ingredients
1 tomato
½ red bell pepper
½ cup organic corn
½ cucumber
1 clove garlic
1 cup water
2 limes, juiced
½ teaspoon sea salt
½ teaspoon cumin
½ teaspoon chili powder
½ teaspoon paprika
Small handful of cilantro leaves
½ avocado
1 teaspoon chili flakes

Directions
Blend all ingredients on high for 40 seconds or until smooth. Save any leftovers for your next smoothie or reserve it for the next day.

Spicy Strawberry Lemonaide

Turmeric has been used in India for more than 2,500 years for its medicinal health benefits. Cancer and other chronic diseases are less often seen in India versus the Western countries with use of this powerful root. It is also a natural liver detoxifier, prevents and stops the growth of prostate cancer, removes amyloid plaque in the brain, which causes Alzheimer's, is an anti-inflammatory that helps alleviate arthritis, and slows the progression of multiple sclerosis.

Ingredients
1 cup coconut water
1 cup frozen strawberries
¼–½ inch turmeric root
2 lemons, juiced
2 tablespoons honey or agave
10 ice cubes

Directions
Blend all ingredients on high for 40 seconds or until smooth.

Strawberry Cream

Strawberries curb overeating, maintain regular digestion, and contain antioxidants and vitamin C to lower blood pressure and create a healthy immune system. They are anti-inflammatory, anti-cancer, and contain manganese to help battle those free radicals and oxidative stress.

Ingredients
½ cup nut milk
1 cup frozen strawberries
1 tablespoon vanilla protein powder
½ the beans of a vanilla pod (optional)
½ frozen banana
3 drops stevia

Directions
Blend all ingredients on high for 40 seconds or until smooth.

Strawberry Cheesecake

The powerful maca root was first discovered among the Incans to give their warriors incredible strength before battle. It's also a natural libido enhancer, a Viagra alternative, an energy enhancer, and it increases fertility in women. Maca combats aging and allows the body to feel youthful and vibrant.

Ingredients
2 cups frozen strawberries
1 cup coconut milk kefir
1 tablespoon vanilla protein powder
1 tablespoon coconut oil, melted
1 tablespoon maca powder
1–2 tablespoons agave
1 teaspoon nutritional yeast
1 dash cinnamon

Directions
Blend all ingredients for 40 seconds or until smooth.

Strawberry Shortcake

Lower your cholesterol with a big glass of strawberry shortcake. Strawberries are proven to lower the amount of low-density lipoprotein, which leads to bad cholesterol, and contains phytonutrients and antioxidants to help prevent cancer.

Ingredients
2 cups frozen strawberries
2 cups almond milk
1 tablespoon vanilla protein powder
1 tablespoon coconut oil, melted
1 tablespoon maca powder

Directions
Blend all ingredients on high for 40 seconds or until smooth. Drink it just the way it is or create layers of strawberry shortcake and nondairy whipped cream topped with a few sliced strawberries.

Sunkist Cold Reducer

Boost your immune system and kick that cold in the butt with an excellent source of vitamin C and flavonoids, which help to prevent the common cold and throat infections. Tangelos can also aid in treating urinary tract infections, respiratory-related problems, such as asthma and bronchitis, the prevention of premature aging, and they prevent damage that free radicals can cause upon the body.

Ingredients
½ cup hazelnut milk
½ cup almond milk
2 tangelos, peeled and seeded
1 tablespoon vanilla protein powder
½ frozen banana
1 tablespoon coconut syrup

Directions
Blend all ingredients on high for 40 seconds or until smooth.

Sweet Potato Pie

Are you diabetic and miss eating white potatoes, rice, and flour? While these foods cause blood sugar levels to spike, the cute little sweet potato will slowly absorb glucose and sustain it at a moderate level, then return it to a regular level gradually. Try the naturally sweet, low-glycemic sweet potato packed with essential vitamins A, C, and B6. Not only is it great for diabetics, but the phytonutrients can reduce inflammation and detoxify by lowering free radicals and heavy metals in the body, easing persons who have irritable bowel syndrome (IBS) and digestive disorders.

Ingredients
1 carrot, juiced
1 sweet potato, juiced
½ teaspoon maca
¼ cup almond milk
¼ teaspoon cinnamon
½ pinch ginger
1 teaspoon agave
½ teaspoon vanilla protein powder
8 ice cubes

Directions
Blend all ingredients on high for 40 seconds or until smooth.

Sweet Tart

Fight cancer and alleviate arthritis with this delicious fruit. Extinguish cancer cells for good with ellagic acid (a phytonutrient compound) and quercetin (which is present in raspberries) that kill certain types of cancer, according to the Cancer Prevention Research Study published in 2010. Raspberries turn off the signals that create an inflammatory response in the body.

Ingredients
1 cup frozen raspberries
2 limes, juiced
1 tablespoon coconut oil, melted
½ frozen banana
1½ cups water
½ cup hemp milk

Directions
Blend all ingredients on high for 40 seconds or until smooth.

Fat Melting V8

Burn those calories and fat away without stepping foot in the gym. Sweet red pepper contains capsaicin, which is an ingredient in many weight-loss pills and supplements. Capsaicin is also contained in topical pain-relief creams for its anti-inflammatory properties. Chili peppers were used more than seven thousand years ago in Central America and Mexico for the great healing properties they contain: they can relieve migraines, fight against sinus infections, reduce cholesterol, lower the chance of heart attack and stroke, treat arthritis, psoriasis, and eliminate body fat.

Ingredients
2 tomatoes
2 red chili peppers
½ celery stalk
1 lime, juiced
1 cup water
½ teaspoon sea salt and pepper

Directions
Blend all ingredients on high for 40 seconds or until smooth.

Zucchini Nut Bread

Adding sprouts—a superfood—to your diet will help build your immune function, nerve tissue, bones, and blood. Sprouts fight disease and nourish cells with their high antioxidant-rich support and tons of enzymes and protein. A diet consisting of high antioxidants will neutralize free radicals, which are damaging to the inside of the body because they destroy enzymes. Enzymes are essential for breathing, kidney and liver function, and digestion as they break down foods and the phytic acid we consume. Antioxidants can protect us from toxic overload.

Ingredients
1 cup hemp milk
1 cup zucchini, chopped
½ frozen banana
½ cup walnuts
1 tablespoon vanilla protein powder
1 teaspoon agave
1 teaspoon cinnamon
Small handful of alfalfa or clover sprouts

Directions
Blend all ingredients, except sprouts, on high for 40 seconds or until smooth.
Top with sprouts.

Squash the Fat

Squash the fat and burn more calories by replacing a high-calorie meal with only 40 calories per one cup of squash, making your weight-loss goals more attainable while exercising. Enhance your immunity with carotenes (which are contained in the deep, golden color of squash); lower your risk of lung cancer and emphysema with high levels of vitamin A and beta-cryptoxanthin; lower your risk of cancer, high blood pressure, diabetes, and heart disease with omega-3 fatty acids; and create one of the best catalysts to improve calcium absorption in the body with magnesium.

Ingredients
1 cup frozen raw butternut squash, peeled and diced
1½ cups almond milk
¼ cup coconut water
1 teaspoon cinnamon
1 teaspoon vanilla protein powder
6 ice cubes

Directions
Blend all ingredients on high for 40 seconds or until smooth.

Matcha Madness

The crazy matcha green leaf is packed with rich chlorophyll and is superior in its effects for blood detoxification, mood enhancement, energy-boosting, stress-reducing, combating inflammation, oxidation and aging, mind clarity and alertness, and immunity-boosting. It has powerful anticarcinogenic properties, a high fiber content, and contains more antioxidants than a cup of green tea or goji berries. It may also lower cholesterol and lower blood pressure. If that isn't enough, try drinking this Matcha Madness before a workout and melt 25 percent more of that stubborn body fat.

Ingredients
1 teaspoon matcha
½ cup warm water
1 cup hemp milk
½ banana
1 tablespoon vanilla protein powder
1 cup spinach
¼ teaspoon maca
1 tablespoon agave
10 ice cubes

Directions
Place 1 teaspoon matcha in ½ cup of warm water and whisk well.
Place all remaining ingredients, along with the matcha liquid, into a blender and mix on high for 40 seconds or until smooth. Top with nondairy cream.

Sweet and Spicy Apple

Ease any nausea, motion sickness, menstrual cramps, and muscle soreness with the amazing benefits of ginger. Not only does this tiny root have anti-inflammatory properties, but it also promotes proper digestion for IBS sufferers, reduces headache symptoms, and helps to manage type-2 diabetes, and slow cancer growth.

Ingredients
1 medium-sized carrot
1 small Gala or Fuji apple, cored and chopped
1-inch ginger knuckle
1–1½ cups water
6 ice cubes

Directions
Blend all ingredients on high for 40 seconds or until smooth.

Cress the Tropics

Watercress is one of the most nutrient dense vegetables known to man. It has been used for ages as a therapeutic aphrodisiac. This medicinal herb will provide the bones with more calcium than milk and more iron than spinach, making it very effective in persons with anemia and osteoporosis. The combination of iron with vitamin C helps the body to readily absorb iron, while milk's calcium will actually block the absorption of iron.

Watercress contains antioxidants to fight the damaging effects of free radicals in the body. How great is that? Even persons with diabetes will benefit from the high soluble fiber that reduces the absorption of carbohydrates in the body. Watercress has so many more health benefits: removes toxins from the body, cures gingivitis, prevents goiter, alleviates dandruff, improves eye health, improves digestive function, treats chronic bronchitis with its sulphur glycosides, and promotes strong bones. It is an anti-cancer superfood to say the least.

How can you incorporate watercress? Add it to sandwiches, salads, soups, or raw vegan pizza. Incorporate this vegetable into your diet today, and give your body the needed essential nutrients it's been craving.

Ingredients
2 cups spinach packed
1 cup water
⅓ cup watercress
½ avocado
8 ice cubes

Directions
Blend all ingredients on high for 40 seconds or until smooth.

Milky Way

Real maple syrup contains fewer calories and has a high concentration of zinc and manganese, which contains not only marked enzymes to create energy, but also fifty-four antioxidant factors that can prevent or delay diseases caused by free radicals which can cause cancer, diabetes, and atherosclerosis. Both zinc and manganese work in conjunction with each other to create a healthy immune system, lessening the inflammation in the body.

Ingredients
1 tablespoon chocolate protein powder
1 teaspoon vanilla protein power
1 cup almond milk
1 tablespoon coconut oil, melted
1 tablespoon almond butter
1 tablespoon cocoa powder
1 tablespoon maple syrup
1 teaspoon cocoa nibs, crushed
8 ice cubes

Directions
Blend all ingredients, except cocoa nibs, on high for 40 seconds or until smooth. Top with cocoa nibs for a great chocolaty crunch with each sip.

Green Apple Pie

At last, if you suffer from celiac disease or have gluten intolerance, you can enjoy oats, too. Adding these gluten-free rolled oats to your diet will help you feel fuller longer, providing energy and reducing the risk of type-2 diabetes with the presence of beta-glucan, a soluble fiber that controls blood sugar and slows the absorption of sugar during digestion while lowering bad cholesterol. Although oats are beneficial, it is important to soak them for several hours or preferably overnight. The outer layer of the bran contains phytic acid, which will bind to essential minerals and block their absorption, making persons more prone to irritable bowel syndrome. Presoaking the oats will break down and neutralize the phytic acid and improve overall benefits!

Ingredients
1 green apple, cored and chopped
¼ cup coconut water
½ cup almond milk
1 tablespoon vanilla protein powder
1 tablespoon gluten-free rolled oats
1 teaspoon maca
⅛ teaspoon cinnamon
1 cup spinach
10 ice cubes

Directions
Blend all ingredients on high for 40 seconds or until smooth.

Coconut Cream Pie

America's new health craze, coconut water, is Mother Nature's sport drink! Coconut water contains electrolytes, is hydrating, low in calorie, fat- and cholesterol-free, and packed full of potassium. If you're an athlete or gym-junkie, this drink is just for you!

Ingredients
½ frozen banana
1 teaspoon maca
½ cup coconut water
⅛ teaspoon fresh ginger
1 tablespoon vanilla protein powder
¼ cup fresh coconut meat or coconut flakes
½ cup coconut milk
8 coconut milk ice cubes

Directions
Blend all ingredients on high for 40 seconds or until smooth.

Green Monkey

Flax contains omega-3 and omega-6 essential fatty acids, which keep the heart healthy. You will see flax in many food products on the market today: crackers, waffles, and oats, to mention a few. Flax contains higher levels of lignans than most other plant foods. Lignans are largely made of phytoestrogens, which are estrogen-like chemicals and act as antioxidants. When consumed, the intestinal bacteria activate the lignans, which have been known to prevent precancerous cell growth and slow down the progression and movement of cancer cells, according to the *British Journal of Nutrition*.

Ingredients
½ cucumber
1 sprig parsley
½ frozen banana
1 cup almond milk
1 teaspoon flax seed, crushed
8 ice cubes

Directions
Blend all ingredients on high for 40 seconds or until smooth.

Lemon Meringue Pie

This has got to be one of my favs! The refreshing zesty kick of lemon truly makes this smoothie special. For years, traditional Ayurvedic treatments in India have used lemon grass for fever remedies. Used as an essential oil, it can restore and revitalize the body, relieving headaches, body aches and pains and calming stress. A popular name for lemon grass is citronella, which is used in candles, perfumes, and soap.

The leaves contain folic acid, vitamins B6, B1, C, A, potassium, zinc, calcium, iron, manganese, copper, and magnesium. Wow! Another great superfood. It's used in tea as a diuretic, helping to flush out toxins. Other uses are for cough and cold symptoms, digestion, constipation, insomnia, type-2 diabetes, and cholesterol.

Ingredients
1 lemon grass stalk
1 lime, juiced
½ cup coconut water
1 frozen banana
½ cup almond milk
6 ice cubes

Directions
Remove outer layers from the lemon grass stalk and use softer core. Chop it into small slices and place in the blender with all ingredients on high for 40 seconds or until smooth.

Garlic Lover

Are you prone to the cold and flu easily throughout the year? According to a study by the University of Maryland Medical Center, persons who consume raw garlic experience fewer colds and/or shorter duration of infections due to the antibacterial and antiviral properties garlic contains. Instead of grabbing medication for a cold, next time eat raw garlic and boost your immunity naturally. When garlic is cooked, it loses the ability to make allicin, which has many health benefits, including the prevention of cancer.

Ingredients
½ lemon, juiced
1–2 garlic cloves, depending on how much *POW!* you crave
½ cucumber, peeled
½ teaspoon rosemary
½ teaspoon thyme
½ cup presoaked cashews
1 cup almond milk
8 ice cubes

Directions
Blend all ingredients on high for 40 seconds or until smooth. Top with a light dash of sea salt, a few tiny slices of cucumber, and a sprinkle of thyme and rosemary.

Licorice Lime Slush

Fennel originated in the Mediterranean and has been used for culinary and medicinal purposes. It grows along the coastal climates and riverbanks and has a distinct black licorice taste. As a kid, I used to pull a few stems off wild plants and just start chewing it. *Mmmmm.* Now, I've come to find out it has a multitude of benefits; it relieves anemia, indigestion, bad breath, flatulence, and constipation. It also contains potassium to reduce blood pressure and helps brain function and cognitive abilities. Potassium is an electrolyte that is a catalyst to increase electrical conduction within the body, including connections within the brain.

Ingredients
2 dates, pitted
½ cup water + 1 cup water
1 cup fennel with leaves and stem
1 lime, juiced
½ celery stalk
8–10 ice cubes

Directions
Chop and soak pitted dates in ½ cup water for 20 minutes, drain, and add to blender with all other ingredients on high for 40 seconds or until smooth.

Kalerd Island

If you're lactose intolerant, you may wonder how to get your calcium. Although kale doesn't have as much calcium as cow's milk, it does not contain the same amount of saturated fat. Plus, the added vitamin C will help calcium absorb more readily than cow's milk.

Per the US National Library of Medicine, National Institutes of Health, kale is a member of the brassica family and contains glucosinolates, an anticarcinogenic. Kale encourages the production of enzymes in the liver that detoxify cancer-causing chemicals. Sulforaphane is also contained in kale, which prevents cancer by shutting off the gene associated with promoting abnormal cells into cancer cells. Maybe you're not a big fan of kale, but with this recipe, you won't even taste it. Reap the benefits and reduce your risk of cancer by consuming more cruciferous vegetables.

Ingredients
1 cup water
1 cup pineapple
1 kale leaf
1 tablespoon vanilla protein powder
8 ice cubes

Directions
Blend all ingredients on high for 40 seconds or until smooth.

Banana Cream Pie

Fifteen pecan halves are equal in protein to one ounce of meat. The buttery sweet taste of pecans makes any dish delectable, and this smoothie takes the cake, providing antioxidant activity, vitamin E, beta-carotene, lutein, and zeaxanthin, which removes toxic free radicals and protects the body from cancer, disease, and infections. Pecans also provide vitamin B-complex groups: riboflavin, niacin, thiamin, pantothenic acid, and folates, which aid in enzyme metabolism within the body. They also contain manganese, potassium, calcium, iron, magnesium, zinc, and selenium. All these essential levels of minerals, vitamins, and protein fight heart disease, reduce high cholesterol, and prevent heart attacks.

Ingredients
2 dates, pitted
¼ cup pecans
½ cup coconut water
½ cup almond milk
1 large frozen banana
¼ teaspoon maca

Directions
Chop and soak pitted dates along with pecans in ½ cup coconut water for 20 minutes. Then add the dates, pecans, and coconut water to the blender, along with all other ingredients on high for 40 seconds or until smooth.

Alkalinity

A powerhouse of alkaline foods will fuel your body if you're feeling a toxic overload. If you've been traveling or feel overworked, rejuvenate your health with alkalinity. Every ingredient will restore energy, mental clarity, and give your body every vitamin, mineral, healthy carb, fiber, and the nutrition it needs to quickly recover from the fast-paced life that deprives your body. Don't take your health for granted; it needs tender loving care. And this smoothie is just the pill your body is craving and deserves.

Ingredients
½ lemon, juiced
2 heaping cups spinach
½ cucumber
1 sprig parsley
Sliver of beet
1 garlic clove
½ cup water
10 ice cubes

Directions
Blend all ingredients on high for 40 seconds or until smooth.

Almond Butter Cup

Want a sweet treat without the guilt? Look no further. This smoothie treat won't raise blood sugar levels. According to the *Nutrition Journal*, dates are a low-glycemic index food. This sweet date has the ability to lower cholesterol levels, lowering your risk of the hardening of arteries, stroke, and heart attack, as reported by the National Institutes of Health. Dates contain vitamin B6, K, and A, potassium, copper, manganese, magnesium, calcium, phosphorous, iron, and zinc.

Ingredients
1 date, pitted
¼ cup coconut water
1 tablespoon cocoa
1 tablespoon chocolate protein powder
1 teaspoon tahini (optional)
1 tablespoon almond butter
¾ cup almond milk
10 ice cubes

Directions
Soak pitted date in ¼ cup coconut water for 20 minutes. Then add both the date and coconut water to the blender, along with all other ingredients on high for 40 seconds or until smooth.

Sour Power

Get ready to pucker-up, sour lovers. This smoothie is bursting with outrageous flavor. The cranberries improve your circulatory system, relieve asthma symptoms, plus reduce bacteria in the urinary tract, alleviating urinary tract infections.

Ingredients
8 frozen strawberries
½ cup cranberries
1 cup cashew milk
3 ice cubes
½ lime, juiced

Directions
Blend all ingredients on high for 40 seconds or until smooth.

Peanut Butter Cinnamon Toast

This smoothie is a great start to any morning, filling your tummy for hours. Cashews are rich in calcium, necessary for strong bones, magnesium for bone growth, and copper for vital functioning of enzymes to aid in combining collagen and elastin, therefore providing flexibility in bones and joints.

Ingredients
1 tablespoon peanut butter
1 cup cashew milk
1 frozen banana
1 teaspoon vanilla protein powder
½ teaspoon cinnamon
⅛ teaspoon maca

Directions
Blend all ingredients on high for 40 seconds or until smooth. You may opt to save the cinnamon for a nice topping instead of blending it all within the smoothie. Either way, it's delish!

Treasure Chest

Avast, ye mateys! This green smoothie is only for those seasoned green-lovin' pirates. The smoothness from the avocado and the sour kick from the lime will get your taste buds salivating. Add a bit of moringa leaf, and you're off with boundless energy! Moringa is known as the Tree of Life, containing ninety nutrients, including forty antioxidants, has the highest protein ratio of any other plant studied so far on Earth, and contains all eight essential amino acids for proper protein synthesis.

The benefits of moringa include: increasing the immune system, promoting cell structure, stabilizing diabetes, reducing inflammation, neutralizing toxins, and promoting proper digestion. It is also an amazing energy booster, natural anxiety suppressant, and does so much more. If you're new to moringa, start with ¼ teaspoon for up to five days, every other day, and increase to 1 teaspoon over time. Ease into it s-l-o-w-l-y! It's potent, and your body needs to adapt to gain the benefits. If you are on blood-thinning medication or pregnant, consult your physician before taking moringa.

Ingredients
½ avocado
2 cups spinach
½–1 lime, juiced
¼ teaspoon moringa leaf powder
⅓ cup coconut water
½ cup water
6–8 ice cubes

Directions
Blend all ingredients on high for 40 seconds or until smooth.

Nilla Berry

While the coconut water contains no refined sugars, it is pure sweetness all on its own; it is a natural source of hydration and contains essential electrolytes. Add cranberries to the punch, and you've got yourself a low-calorie sports drink to improve the body's circulatory system.

Ingredients
¼ cup cranberries
1 green apple, cored and chopped
¾ cup cashew milk
¼ cup coconut water
1 teaspoon vanilla protein powder
½ frozen banana
10 ice cubes

Directions
Blend all ingredients on high for 40 seconds or until smooth.

Keep It Simple

This smoothie is for juicing enthusiasts, not for the sweet cravers. It's just something simple and clean to whip up when your produce is running low in the fridge and you're in a hurry. Never use traditional table salt that has been stripped of essential minerals; that leads to dehydration and high blood pressure, among other problems. Add a bit of sea salt to the mix, and you've got eighty additional unrefined minerals needed for the body, some of which include magnesium, potassium, calcium, and other nutrients.

Ingredients
½ cucumber
½ carrot
1 tomato
½ cup water
⅛ teaspoon thyme
⅛ teaspoon sea salt
6 ice cubes

Directions
Blend all ingredients on high for 40 seconds or until smooth.

Tart & Crisp Chayote

Chayote is a good source of amino acids, vitamin C, diuretics, antioxidants, and has high anti-inflammatory properties. It also has folate, which is good for the heart; copper, which keeps thyroid healthy; zinc, which prevents acne, controls the production of oil in the skin; vitamin K, which prevents bone loss; potassium, which reduces blood pressure; vitamin B6, which is good for the brain and improves memory; magnesium, which prevents muscle cramps; and manganese, which helps the body convert protein and fat into energy.

Chayote can be eaten raw, marinated lightly with citrus juice and sea salt if desired. It has a mild flavor and tastes like something between a pear and a cucumber.

Ingredients
½ chayote
1 green apple, cored and chopped
1 celery stalk
1 cup water
⅛ cup coconut water
Small wedge of lemon, juiced
6 ice cubes (optional)

Directions
Blend all ingredients on high for 40 seconds or until smooth.

Dark Chocolate Brownie

Surprisingly delicious and naturally sweet, raw cacao is high in antioxidants and flavonoids, which promote cardiovascular health, reduce blood clotting, and improve circulation and blood pressure. It also improves your mood by increasing the levels of serotonin and endorphins in the brain.

Ingredients
2 dates, pitted
¼ cup pecans
½ cup coconut milk
1 cup almond milk
2 tablespoons cocoa powder or raw cacao powder
1 tablespoon agave
1 tablespoon chocolate protein powder
8 ice cubes
Pinch of sea salt

Directions
Chop pitted dates and place in coconut milk, along with pecans, and soak for 20 minutes. Add soaked dates, pecans, and coconut milk, along with all other ingredients into blender on high for 40 seconds or until smooth.

Carrot Cake

Raisins are loaded with natural sweetness, while the kefir—a probiotic—mimics the taste of the sour cream frosting to a delicious carrot cake. Did you know that protein bars are just glorified candy bars? Most contain more than 10 grams of sugar and have ingredients you can't even pronounce. For the bodybuilding enthusiast, instead of opting for a power bar, grab a handful of raisins or drink a Carrot Cake smoothie to promote energy, aid in digestion, enhance bone health with the rich source of calcium, reduce acidity levels within the body, and promote your libido with the amino acid arginine found in raisins.

Ingredients
¼ cup raisins
¼ cup milk kefir
½ frozen banana
2 large carrots
Sliver of ginger root
1 cup coconut milk
¼ teaspoon cinnamon
1 teaspoon vanilla protein powder

Directions
Chop raisins and place in kefir
and soak for 20 minutes. Add raisins and kefir, along with all other ingredients into blender on high for 40 seconds or until smooth. You may also opt to juice the carrot and add 6 ice cubes to the smoothie.

The Dandelion

One cup of chopped dandelion greens contain more calcium than kale, is rich in iron, loaded with antioxidants, vitamins A, C, B1, B2, B6, E, K, and is a must for your green smoothies to help detox and cleanse the liver. This recipe calls for five dandelion greens. Work your way up to more greens each time and double the health benefits; the more the better!

Ingredients
5 dandelion greens
½ avocado
1 cup coconut water
1 cup water
1 mint leaf (optional)
Pinch of sea salt

Directions
Blend all ingredients on high for 40 seconds or until smooth and pour over ice.

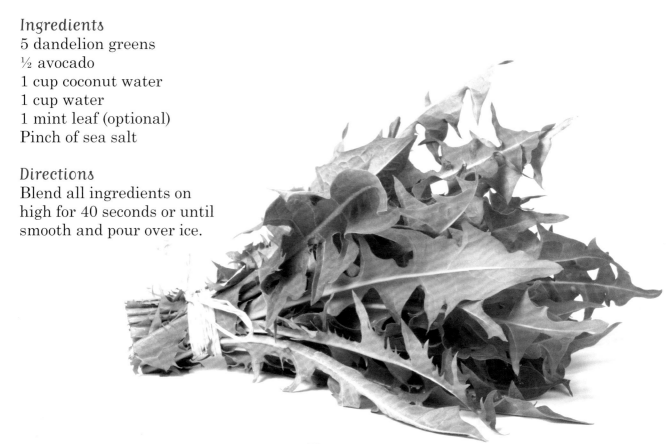

100 Calorie Detoxifier

Enjoy the third most expensive spice in the world, cardamom, with its amazing medicinal properties. Originating from India, this warm spice has been used to cleanse the body; improve blood circulation, digestion, heartburn, intestinal spasms, irritable bowel syndrome (IBS), intestinal gas, constipation, liver and gallbladder complaints, and loss of appetite; relieve acidity in the stomach; cure halitosis; and ease a sore throat. It is also used for the common cold, cough, bronchitis and to prevent infection.

Cardamom contains chemicals that appear to treat stomach and intestinal spasms and gas and increase the movement of food through the intestine.

If you've been out in the hot afternoon sun and nothing seems to quench your thirst, it may just be that your electrolyte levels are low, which makes it nearly impossible for your kidneys to hold on to water and all is lost through the urine. Hydrate and balance your electrolytes with coconut water by sipping on this restorative, cool, refreshing smoothie.

Ingredients
½ banana
¾ cup coconut water
½ lemon, juiced
15 ice cubes
¼ teaspoon cardamom

Directions
Blend all ingredients on high for 40 seconds or until smooth.

Plum Pudding

Do you suffer from diverticulitis and can't stand the thought of eating prunes every day for the rest of your life? Look no further. Dried plums are called prunes, and with the added chia seeds, you will get all the dietary fiber needed to relieve constipation, which may result in diverticulitis symptoms. Plus, prunes are a great source of antioxidant compounds, contain thiamine, riboflavin, calcium, iron, potassium, magnesium, vitamins B, vitamin K which is essential to proteins involved in blood coagulation, and vitamin A which aids in healthy vision. Add kefir to the mix, and it will help restore your gut flora.

Ingredients
4 dried moist plums/prunes
½ cup coconut milk kefir
1 tablespoon chia seeds
½ cup cashew milk
4 frozen strawberries
½ frozen banana
⅛ teaspoon cinnamon
⅛ teaspoon fresh ginger
½ teaspoon vanilla protein powder

Directions
Chop dried moist plums/prunes into tiny pieces and soak in kefir, along with chia seeds for 20 minutes. Place plums/prunes, milk kefir, and chia in blender with all ingredients on high for 40 seconds or until smooth.

Rosemary

With its mild, smooth taste and hint of rosemary, this is a great start to incorporating greens into your diet. Rosemary will improve memory, enhance mood, and detoxify the liver by reducing cirrhosis. It's also an anti-inflammatory, anticarcinogenic, antibacterial, immunity builder and is a mild diuretic that can help alleviate bloating and water retention.

Ingredients
1½ cups water
2 celery stalks
6 dandelion greens
¼ small avocado
½ teaspoon rosemary
1 lime wedge, juiced

Directions
Blend all ingredients on high for 40 seconds or until smooth.

Beet It

This is for beet lovers only. Beets have no trans-fats, no saturated fats, and are low in calories, which fills you up and satiates sweet cravings. Beets also help cleanse the blood and colon. They contain calcium, iron, magnesium, phosphorous, niacin, vitamins C and A, and folic acid, which is important for the growth of new cells. The big added bonus is they can prevent several kinds of cancers and heart problems.

Ingredients
1 beet
¼ inch ginger root
½ red apple, cored and chopped
1 cup cashew milk

Directions
Blend all ingredients on high for 40 seconds or until smooth. This recipe is best using a high-speed blender. If you don't own one, you can juice the beet first before adding it to the rest of the ingredients in the blender.

Blackberry Fresca

If you're looking to lose weight and craving fruits, blackberries are your best friend. One cup of blackberries contains 60 calories and 30 percent of recommended dietary fiber to keep you feeling full longer. They promote proper digestive functioning, regulate blood sugar levels, and regulate bowel regularity, plus contain vitamin C, which promotes the development of bones and connective tissues and will boost your overall energy, and vitamin K to help bone proteins and the proteins used to activate blood clotting.

Ingredients
1 cup frozen blackberries
1 tablespoon vanilla protein powder
1 cup coconut water
Half banana

Directions
Blend all ingredients on high for 40 seconds or until smooth and pour over ice for a refreshing fresca. You may opt to substitute coconut water for any preferred nut milk or substitute frozen blackberries for fresh. Either way, this smoothie is the bomb!

Earth Cleanse

Diatomaceous earth will rid your body of junk by attracting E. coli, heavy metals, intestinal worms or parasites, and any other unwanted material in the intestines, absorbing them and flushing them out of your body. The rewards: regular bowel movements, clear skin, stronger and faster growing hair and nails, a healthier colon, and this results in proper nutrients being absorbed more readily in the blood stream. It also reduces the risk of polyps, cancers, and ulcers. You can add diatomaceous earth to any smoothie for these added cleansing benefits.

Ingredients
1 green granny smith apple, cored and peeled
½ cucumber
1 lime, juiced
1 tablespoon diatomaceous earth (food grade)
1 cup water
½ cup cashew milk
15 ice cubes

Directions
Blend all ingredients on high for
40 seconds or until smooth.

Rad Fast

Do you toss radish greens? Radish greens are the most nutritional part of the plant, containing more vitamin C, calcium, iron, as well as other vitamins than the delicious crisp root itself. Cut the greens off the radish, wash, and add to salads, sandwiches, or any green smoothie.

Ingredients
½ cup radish greens, chopped
¾ cup almond milk
½ cup green seedless grapes
1 small celery stalk
8 ice cubes

Directions
Blend all ingredients on high for 20 or 40 seconds until smooth. For those who are on a detox fast, blend ingredients for a shorter duration. This smoothie will have a lighter color, and there will be tiny bits of greens to chew on, which will be satisfying. You may opt to use ¾ cup of water and/or swap out the celery for half of a cucumber.

Chocolate-Covered Coconut Macaroons

Fine macaroon coconut is the dried and desiccated white flesh of the coconut, with natural sweetness packed full of fiber and protein. Instead of grabbing that sweet macaroon cookie you long for, opt for a better alternative dessert, the Chocolate-Covered Coconut Macaroon Smoothie, 100 percent natural with no additives, preservatives, or processed sugar.

Ingredients
⅓ cup fine macaroon coconut
½ teaspoon maca
1 teaspoon raw cacao powder or cocoa powder
1–1½ cups coconut milk
⅓ cup presoaked pecans
½ frozen banana
1 teaspoon honey
6 ice cubes

Directions
Blend all ingredients on high for 40 seconds or until smooth.

21G Protein Packed

This smoothie is super delicious and powerful! Contains 254 calories and 21 grams of protein. If you're watching your weight, you may want to opt for water instead of almond milk. Hemp hearts are rich and nutty in flavor, containing extra protein for those on a vegan diet.

Ingredients

1 cup spinach
2 tablespoons vanilla protein powder
2 cups unsweetened almond milk
1 tablespoon raw hulled hemp seeds
1 tablespoon maca
1 teaspoon acacia fiber powder (optional)

Directions

Blend all ingredients on high for 40 seconds or until smooth.

Bourbon Vanilla Snickerdoodle

Ingredients

1 bourbon vanilla bean
1 cup cashew milk
1 frozen banana
¼ teaspoon cinnamon
1 teaspoon maca powder
4 dates, pitted
2 tablespoons almond butter
4–6 cashew milk ice cubes
1 tablespoon oats (optional)
Garnish with a few cashew pieces

Directions

Slice the vanilla pod lengthwise and use a small sharp paring knife to scrape out the seeds. Add them to the blender with all other ingredients, except cashew pieces, and blend for 40 seconds or until smooth;garnish with cashews, a lil' something to munch on!

Spicy Hot Chaga Milk

Ingredients

2 cups warm Chaga tea*
¼ cup cashews
¼ teaspoon vanilla bean powder
1 tablespoon agave
1 tablespoon cocoa powder
Dash cayenne
Garnish with nondairy coconut whipped cream and cocoa powder**

Directions

Prepare Chaga tea by placing 2 Chaga mushroom chunks per 2 cups water in a small saucepan; simmer on the stovetop for 1 hour to allow for maximum nutrient extraction. Add cashews to the simmering Chaga tea, allowing to soak the full hour; this softens the nuts, releases the enzyme inhibitors, and creates a smoother Spicy Hot Chaga Milk.

Discard Chaga chunks or refrigerate them for up to three uses. Blend Chaga tea, soaked cashews and all other ingredients on high for 40 seconds or until smooth.

Top with homemade coconut whipped cream and a sprinkle of cocoa powder, if desired.

*Main Chaga Tea Chunks from My Berry Organics were used in this recipe; you may opt to prepare several cups in advance, per package instructions, in the slow cooker and refrigerated for up to several days.

**Coconut whipped cream recipe can be found on page 10.

Hot Damn Bloody Mary

For hot and spicy lovers only! Red peppers contain capsaicin, which is an ingredient in many weightloss pills and supplements. Capsaicin is also contained in topical pain relief creams because it relieves migraines, fights against sinus infections, reduces cholesterol, lowers the chance of heart attack and stroke, treats arthritis, psoriasis, eliminates body fat, and possesses anti-inflammatory properties.

Ingredients

1 large tomato
2 celery stalks
3 Red Fresno Peppers, stems and seeds removed
½ cup water
¼ teaspoon chipotle seasoning
1–2 dashes cayenne powder
2 dashes chili powder
2 pinches sea salt

Directions

Blend all ingredients on high for 40 seconds or until smooth.

Pineapple Express

After an intense workout, muscles get pretty much zapped of potassium; which is a primary electrolyte needed to transport glucose into the muscle cells. The depletion of potassium may cause nausea, muscle weakness, cramping, increased heart rate, and slower reflexes. Muscle cells will recover quicker by consuming bananas post-workout. Bromelain, an enzyme contained in pineapples, will also help prevent muscle soreness and inflammation.

Ingredients

1 cup fresh pineapple
⅔ cup almond milk
1 frozen banana
⅓ cup lemon, juiced
¼ teaspoon cinnamon (optional)

Directions

Blend all ingredients on high for 40 seconds or until smooth.

Strawberry Rhubarb

If you're used to sweet smoothies and want to start tapering off sugar, this is a great breakfast smoothie to try for its low glycemic index with coconut sugar. Remember them good ol' days sipping on Strawberry Nesquik and milk? This is very similar in taste, but without the added preservatives and calories. Rhubarb contains calcium, lutein, Vitamin K, and antioxidants.

Ingredients

6 fresh strawberries, hulled
1 rhubarb stalk
1 teaspoon vanilla protein powder
½–1 teaspoon coconut sugar
1 cup almond milk
Dash cinnamon

Directions

Blend all ingredients on high for 40 seconds or until smooth. Pour over ice.

Pecan & Mushroom Soup

The magical mushroom—a natural angiogenesis inhibitor—contains letcins that bind to cancerous and infected cells, giving our immune system a direct road map to identify and destroy the target; ratifying our body of harmful carcinogens.

Ingredients

1 cup vegetable broth
¼ cup dried Porcini mushrooms
¼ cup pecans
¼ cup yellow onion
1 cup (approx. 4 or 5) baby bella mushrooms
½ cup coconut milk
1 teaspoon thyme
1 garlic clove
¼ teaspoon sea salt

Directions

Soak dried Porcini mushrooms and pecans in vegetable broth for 15 minutes; pour into blender, with all other ingredients and blend on high for 40 to 90 seconds, depending on your desired consistency. Pour into a serving bowl and sip as a soup.

Testimonials

"Michelle understands how to combine foods to create the wow factor. Her smoothies are nutritionally dense, flavorful, and beautifully presented. She truly has a gift."
—Melissa Kubek
liteBOD Health & Energy, litebod.com

"Michelle's recipes are so full of life that your body and taste buds will think you're having a party. They are easy to prepare even for the novice cook, like me, and are a treat for the whole family. They make a vegan lifestyle simple to adopt. When Michelle cooks, you can feel the love in each bite and even when you make the recipes yourself, the love comes through. Thank you with all my heart, Michelle."
—Sunita Shinde

"My wife and I used to eat whatever we wanted and felt high and low and sleepy after a food coma. Now that we're in the process of following The Green Aisle detox, we feel more focused with choices in life, at work and with our baby. We both sleep easier and feel that we can wake up without snoozing the alarm anymore. Thank you!"
—Hovo and Adelina Nazaryan

"Michelle is amazing at putting together tastes and food designs! She has a natural ability to make the tastebuds wake up, and her foods are a culinary delight and healthy too!"
—Karen Brake

"I had tried everything to lose weight and feel better, to no avail. Then Michelle introduced me to juicing and a healthier way of eating. I have lost a considerable amount of weight, and I feel terrific for the first time in a long time. And I don't feel deprived at all. Most people don't realize there are a lot of healthy foods that are just as satisfying and don't pack the pounds on. There are no fast and easy ways to lose weight. It has to be a lifestyle change. Michelle has taught me so much about combining the right foods and just what to eat to help with weightloss. And I've kept it off, too.

"Michelle's recipes are always fast and easy to make. The best thing about her recipes, though, is they offer something new and different instead of eating the same old thing. She has introduced me to so many different foods that I never would have tried on my own, and she explains what each food does for your body. Finally, interesting recipes that are good for your body and that taste great."
—Carol Paradise

"As a health coach I'm always looking for healthy material to recommend to my clients and this book definitely supports good health! In the beginning, this book has some great information on healthy eating and food in general. Then, dive into some great recipes that will refresh and you healthy! I give this book to all of the clients in my program, highly recommend it!"
—Steven Loeschner, Steve Loeschner LLC, steveloeschner.com

Recipe Index

References

Sources that were influential in the writing and researching of this book include:

books
Brenda Watson, C.N.C., *The Detox Strategy* (Simon & Schuster, Inc., Pub Co: 2008).
Donna Gates with Linda Schatz, *The Body Ecology Diet* (Hay House, Inc., Pub Co: 2011).
Kaayla T. Daniel, PhD, CCN, *The Whole Soy Story* (New Trends Publishing, Inc., Pub Co: 2005).

websites
AMA's campaign against salt fails to recognize health benefits of sea salt and trace minerals, Natural News, Natural Health News & Scientific Discoveries
http://www.naturalnews.com/019680_excess_sodiu_dietary_salt.html

Chlorogenic Acid, Wikipedia
http://en.wikipedia.org/wiki/Chlorogenic_acid

Dangers of Milk and Dairy Products – The Facts
http://rense.com/general26/milk.htm

Disposable coffee cups, carryout containers filled with cancer-causing agents, Natural News, Natural Health News & Scientific Discoveries
http://www.naturalnews.com/032732_styrofoam_chemicals.html

Drinking water with meals can impair digestion, Natural News, Natural Health News & Scientific Discoveries
http://www.naturalnews.com/033731_digestion_drinking_water.html

Health Dangers of Table Salt, Global Healing Center, Natural Health & Organic Living
http://www.globalhealingcenter.com/natural-health/dangers-of-salt/

Hungry for Change
http://www.hungryforchange.tv/article/sneaky-names-for-msg-check-your-labels
http://prophesyagain.org/msg-hidden-in-plain-sight-its-new-claim-to-fame/
http://breakingmuscle.com/nutrition/almost-magic-why-you-need-to-eat-more-mushrooms

Marketing Milk and Disease, John McDougall, MD, Newsletter
http://www.nealhendrickson.com/mcdougall/030500pudairyanddisease.htm

Nutrition: Medicine of the Future
http://www.trans4mind.com/nutrition/nutrition.pdf

Six Tips to Reduce The Stress Hormone, Cortisol, Teecino
http://teeccino.com/building_optimal_health/148/Six-Tips-To-Reduce-The-Stress-Hormone,-Cortisol.html

Smarter Living: Chemical Index Styrene, NRDC, National Resources Defense Council
http://www.nrdc.org/living/chemicalindex/styrene.asp

Soy: This "Miracle Health Food" Has Been Linked to Brain Damage and Breast Cancer
http://articles.mercola.com/sites/articles/archive/2010/09/18/soy-can-damage-your-health.aspx

Truth is Treason, pH Levels and Cancer, Alkaline and Acidic Foods
http://www.truthistreason.net/ph-levels-and-cancer-alkaline-and-acidic-foods

When Friends Ask: "Why Don't You Drink Milk?" John McDougall, MD
https://www.drmcdougall.com/misc/2007nl/mar/dairy.htm

Acknowledgments

This wouldn't have been possible without my awesome editor, Nicole Frail from Skyhorse Publishing, for making all things happen!! You rock!

Thank you to . . .

Skyhorse Publishing for making this dream a reality!

Curt and Lynette Smith, my parents, for some creative ideas that helped transform amazing flavors!

Bebe and Scott, my two beautiful children who keep me growing young and my honest little taste testers. Thank you!

Kenny Kaneshiro from CameraShock Photography, for your amazing bio photography shoot and encouragement to never give up on my dreams.

Mae Desmond and Drew Canole from FitLife.tv, my incredible journey into a healthier lifestyle started with you. A special thank-you!

Djamel Bettahar and Spencer Downey Knowlton, my diet and strength training coaches from Weak Bod to Greek God.

Dear close Juicing Sistas: Sunita Shinde, Kaz Bee, Melissa Kubek, and Teri Sharp for your heartfelt support, believing in me, and loves.

Best Friend, Tiffany Chandler, who is always there for me no matter what, with invaluable advice and encouragement.

Mary Lou Sandler for introducing me to The Body Ecology, being an inspiration, and opening my eyes to a new vegan world.

Metric and Imperial Conversions

(These conversions are rounded for convenience)

Ingredient	Cups/Tablespoons/Teaspoons	Ounces	Grams/Milliliters
Protein powder	1 tablespoon	0.3 ounces	8 grams
Coconut flour	1 cup/1 tablespoon	4.5 ounces/ 0.3 ounce	125 grams/8 grams
Fruit, dried	1 cup	4 ounces	120 grams
Fruits or veggies, chopped	1 cup	5 to 7 ounces	145 to 200 grams
Fruits or veggies, puréed	1 cup	8.5 ounces	245 grams
Honey, maple syrup, or agave	1 tablespoon	.75 ounce	20 grams
Liquids: nut milks or water	1 cup	8 fluid ounces	240 milliliters
Gluten-free rolled oats	1 cup	5.5 ounces	150 grams
Salt	1 teaspoon	0.2 ounce	6 grams
Spices: cinnamon, cloves, ginger, or nutmeg (ground)	1 teaspoon	0.2 ounce	5 milliliters
Nut butters	1 cup/1 tablespoon	7 ounces/ 0.5 ounce	200 grams/ 12.5 grams
Vanilla extract	1 teaspoon	0.2 ounce	4 grams

Index